A TOWER BUILT DOWNWARDS

一座向下修建的

T0044217

Before and since his enforced exile from 1989, Y. most innovative and influential poets from China. *A Tower Built Downwards* is the latest instalment of his poetry, written between 2019 and 2022. The different sections – short poems, sequences, and two long poems – form a single comprehensive statement of Yang's recent explorations. It is rooted in his living experience of the historical retrogression of Hong Kong, the disaster of Covid-19, the global spiritual crisis, as well as his personal sadness at events such as the deaths of his father and brother.

The creativity of the writing faces – is even excited by – the depth of the challenges of reality. The long title poem in seven parts is a spiritual journey travelling back in time, completed back in the now, building up into 'a reincarnation within one', as endless time is transformed into multilayered poetical space, in Ai Weiwei's words: 'This intellectual tower... [turns] the unsurpassable puzzles intermingled with life and death into an in-depth exploration of human emotion.'

'In exile from China since 1989's Tiananmen Square massacre, Yang Lian is a writer of world significance; his admirers include Ai Weiwei, who designed the cover of his latest book. Its title evokes the exile's backwards struggle to construct belonging. It also summarises Yang's profound, distinctive verse, which clothes ideas and feelings with details from the lived world. Brilliantly translated by Brian Holton, this substantial collection revisits the poet's personal China, particularly honouring his late father.'
– Fiona Sampson, *The Guardian* (best recent poetry round-up)

'With an introduction and cover by Ai Weiwei, this is Yang Lian's twelfth collection with his long-term translator, Brian Holton. An important poet of the Misty School (banned in China), his poems "grow in the direction of both life and death" (Ai Weiwei), dwelling on the pandemic in Wuhan and the erosion of democracy in Hong Kong. Containing poems rich in image and metaphor, this masterful translation won a PEN Translates Award.'
– Shash Trevett, *Poetry Book Society Bulletin*, Spring 2023

COVER BY AI WEIWEI

Yang Lian was one of the original Misty Poets who reacted against the strictures of the Cultural Revolution. Born in Switzerland, the son of a diplomat, he grew up in Beijing and began writing when he was sent to the countryside in the 1970s. On his return he joined the influential literary magazine *Jintian* (Today). His work was criticised in China in 1983 and formally banned in 1989 when he organised memorial services for the dead of Tiananmen while in New Zealand. He was a Chinese poet in exile from 1989 to 1995, finally settling in London in 1997, also living for some periods in Berlin. Translations of his poetry include five collections with Bloodaxe, *Where the Sea Stands Still* (1999), *Concentric Circles* (2005), *Lee Valley Poems* (2009), *Narrative Poem* (2017) and *A Tower Built Downwards* (2023), as well as his long poem *Yi* (Green Integer, USA, 2002), *Anniversary Snow* (Shearsman, 2019), and *Riding Pisces: Poems from Five Collections* (Shearsman, 2008), a compilation of earlier work. He is co-editor with W.N. Herbert of *Jade Ladder: Contemporary Chinese Poetry* (Bloodaxe Books, 2012), and was awarded the International Nonino Prize in 2012. Both *Where the Sea Stands Still* and *Narrative Poem* are Poetry Book Society Recommended Translations.

Brian Holton was born in Galashiels in the Scottish Border country but grew up partly in Nigeria. After being educated in Greek, French and Latin, he studied Chinese at the universities of Edinburgh and Durham and was the first Programme Director of the Chinese-English/English-Chinese translation programme at Newcastle University. He taught translation for ten years at the Hong Kong Polytechnic University and in 1992 he began a continuing working relationship with the poet Yang Lian, which has so far resulted in a dozen books of translated poetry, including *Where the Sea Stands Still* (Bloodaxe Books, 1999), a Poetry Book Society Recommended Translation, *Concentric Circles* (with Agnes Hung-Chong Chan) (Bloodaxe Books, 2005), *Lee Valley Poems* (with Agnes Hung-Chong Chan and seven poets) (Bloodaxe Books, 2009), *Narrative Poem* (Bloodaxe Books, 2017), *Anniversary Snow* (Shearsman Books, 2019) and *A Tower Built Downwards* (Bloodaxe Books, 2023). He is the lead translator and associate editor of *Jade Ladder: Contemporary Chinese Poetry* (Bloodaxe Books, 2012). He also translates into Scots and is the only currently-publishing Chinese-Scots translator in the world. His latest Chinese-Scots translations are *Hard Roads an Cauld Hairst Winds: Li Bai and Du Fu in Scots* (Taproot Press, 2022) and *Aa Cled Wi Clouds She Cam: Saxty Sang Lyrics* (Irish Pages, 2022).

YANG LIAN
杨炼

A TOWER BUILT
DOWNWARDS
一座向下修建的塔

TRANSLATED BY
BRIAN HOLTON

BLOODAXE BOOKS

ISBN: 978 1 78037 643 1

First published 2023 by
Bloodaxe Books Ltd,
Eastburn,
South Park,
Hexham,
Northumberland NE46 1BS.

www.bloodaxebooks.com
For further information about Bloodaxe titles
please visit our website and join our mailing list
or write to the above address for a catalogue.

This book has been selected to receive financial assistance from English
PEN's PEN Translates programme, supported by Arts Council England.
English PEN exists to promote literature and our understanding of it,
to uphold writers' freedoms around the world, to campaign against the
persecution and imprisonment of writers for stating their views, and to
promote the friendly co-operation of writers and the free exchange of ideas.
www.englishpen.org

Cover design: Neil Astley & Pamela Robertson-Pearce.

Digital reprint of the 2023 Bloodaxe Books edition.

CONTENTS

ACKNOWLEDGEMENTS

This edition contains a complete English translation by Brian Holton of the whole of Yang Lian's 一座向下修建 的塔, *A Tower Built Downwards*. For reasons of censorship in China only part of the work was published there in book form, under the title 在特朗斯特罗默墓前 (At Tranströmer's Grave), by Sichuan People's Publishing House, Chengdu, in 2021. Including some sections would have prevented publication or seen the book banned, the fate of Yang Lian's 敘事詩, *Narrative Poem* (Bloodaxe Books, 2017). Parts of the original Chinese text have also been revised by Yang Lian and this edition is a translation of the final, complete text, with the addition of two new, previously unpublished poems, 'Labyrinth' and 'Anti-requiem'.

Ai Weiwei's introduction which follows was first published as a review of *A Tower Built Downwards* along with Brian Holton's translation of the title-poem in an exhibition catalogue, *Entrelaçar/Intertwine* (Serralves Museum of Contemporary Art, Porto, Portugal, 2022), vol. II, p.73-88. An extract from his translation of the title-poem was also published in *Long Poem Magazine*, Issue 26, Autumn 2021. His translation of 'Touching a Set of Western Zhou Dynasty Bells in Shanghai Museum' was published in *The Poetry Review*, Winter 2022, Volume 112, Issue 4.

INTRODUCTION

Of all the Yang Lian works I have read, *A Tower Built Downwards*, in its intellectual depth, its linguistic forms, and its narrative style, is the most complex and emotionally freighted of his poems. It's like a big tree, growing in the direction of both life and death. It unfolds from a tree and concludes with a tree, using the compound metaphor of tree, human, and tower, to assemble this exegesis of a deep understanding of life. This intellectual tower dives deep down into the loss of his father, individual history, and historical memory, turning the unsurpassable puzzles intermingled with life and death into an in-depth exploration of human emotions.

Yang Lian's language in this poem is mature and unembellished. It brims over as naturally as champagne, it resembles casting metal, or winemaking, as well as blacksmithing, with all kinds of sounds and colours, perfectly blended together into one massive intellectually concentrated poem, a fine poem for which he deserves to be congratulated.

The poetic resources chosen by Yang Lian, such as a Ni Zan painting or an early Shang Dynasty bronze tripod goblet, possess an exquisite aesthetic value. We all know how extremely hard it is to give a metaphysical description of the intrinsic beauty of an object, but that is an extraordinarily easy task for a poet as practised and proficient as he is.

When people have reached an impasse, it is necessarily the case that a turning point will emerge. That happened in the Amazon rainforest, with a great newly-dead 1,200 year-old tree. We duplicated it, copied it, cast it to make a cast-iron artwork 32 metres high and weighing over 40 tons. Such a thing resembles our ship dropping its anchor and hooking on to the rock of the seabed, so that our onward course is most unlikely to be altogether lost. Life is a process of meditation, and even slowly creeping forwards is part of that meditation too.

But back to the poem – in this poem Yang Lian is like a battle-hardened soldier who can see the armour he has shed to return to what is natural: his wounds are clearly visible, and his cast of mind is a touching one. The breath of life can't be blocked, yet sham, hypocritical language does frequently block the breath of life, while genuine, sincere language is utterly naked and exposed, and this is what Yang Lian has accomplished. His existence instantly shows up the true colours of the affectation and artificiality normalised by so many poets, with their contrived moaning and cynical dodging.

Yang Lian's *A Tower Built Downwards* is rigorously and precisely thought through: it links history and reality with metaphysical speculation, as layer by layer it goes deeper and deeper down, until he has transcended tradition, presenting proof of the crimes of human civilisation – while at the same time reading like an accusation of human civilisation. Yang Lian, outstanding logician and analyst, has laid out, dissected, and parsed his evidence for us.

AI WEIWEI
Translated by Brian Holton

A TOWER BUILT DOWNWARDS

一座向下修建的塔

一，短诗

SHORT POEMS

根

Root

Reflections on the life of a work of art
(in response to Ai Weiwei)

1

is this fate?   uprooted   exposed   sun-blasted   charred
forged into iron   iron that day and night growls low

creases flow backwards   skeletons shed from
the figure   clutch an invisible body

the starting point is grotesque   those fingers drag you down
track a set of bronze bells' droning hum stuck to the dead

carved from underground to above ground   wooden labia
keep on cracking open   ghosts hang back at the wooden womb's neck

the end point is grotesque   look back then see
false seasons   false petals

false reincarnation   carrying a point of green on a wooden fingertip
standing tall enough then see   ruin is once only

those internal organs   this heap of flesh-pink rusting stones
pried open emptiness   tightly embedded emptiness

a hand pushes the bells' droning hum   your karma
is here   sunk in the rare flower of death

root   recorded noise of collapse everywhere on its body
there is no creation myth   your last day of life

is here   wearing a million gold-coloured lifejackets
facing the sky to fall into the always bottomless seabed

2

touch yourself and know   the root is in your body
the room a forest   dead tree after dead tree
all say   pain is a luxury
the endless exhibition hall hangs on the hook of the sky
wood at flood tide   slapping   to love pain is an ability
the rippling blue at your side also retells a hole that will choke you
root in your body   and your dried-up desire
decorating the ocean's arabesques wall to wall
the end is everywhere   the drowned are between ends
drifting grotesquely   the starting point has locked up the finish
the endpoint fishes out a beginning from empty internal organs
someone lying on the seabed lies down into the horizon of a bird's nest
to a dead-again shore still not there   you don't need to seek
black   the one and only direction of flow that is woodgrain crying for help
dismantled flesh and blood   a million shiny saws hunt birdsong
tree scars and throats   wildfire held in masturbating gall
on a dry bone   where is your hometown?
lost and lost again   what does shame mean?
you hug a unique history of leaking   the empty sea merely heaves billows
the empty room   emptier once it has caught a man's shadow
endlessly drifting down like a falling leaf   hieroglyph of the dead
write once   invent once
invention   then sinks into unmoving remorse
the root doesn't need to look for me   this seabed comes looking for you
a wooden whirlpool installs the water's depth of someone who stabs sight
dried out aesthetic reproduces as it bares its teeth   your desert likenesses
step in single file into blue brine   shining white draws near lips
smelling a perfume that there's no time can change
is this fate?   you are ruined to become a poem

5 February 2020

致身边消失的陌生人——给武汉

To the Vanished Stranger Beside Us

Written for Wuhan

the sky is bluer than Auschwitz   like a bottle of hand
sanitiser   so closely   balconies guard the field
hear the sound of a bed being shot full of holes
that is where your silhouette sinks   with frosted glass edge
you hold your very last breath   don't believe in final farewells
bit by bit saying farewell to yourself   an exquisitely decorated last will
thrice whitewashed   with coughs   with amazement   with ignorance

a question of suffocation   frozen in the bottom of empty robbed eyes
skin turns transparent   coldly transparent as the air
clotted into a solid untouchable isolation zone everywhere
your life is there   your gas chamber is here
but where are you? where is this perfectly ordinary day?
separation an inch away   has isolated the wailing between two reincarnations
everything happens before your eyes   nothing can be seen

the frosted glass stove door you don't know shuts   tongues of flame
are shut off   in your flesh   in fractured bone the fire you don't know
spits out   incandescent as Valentine's Day   an illusory rose
love   a lie   lives   a rumour
yet who speaks?   that for once rushes off with no last words
with a history unreconciled to vanishing   from within the fire
turn over and sit up   a ghost   unwilling to leave

can't not leave   freezing so many betrayals that take you under armed guard
a destroyed Valentine's Day   who disappeared you?
isolated in the ashes   crowned with shining coloured feelers
small as an emptied-out argument   weightless as a destiny
home is a silhouette   man is a silhouette   howling darkness
nothing can be called back   a mind has to painfully endure deafness
utterly unfamiliar   only then no longer nostalgically recalled

22 February 2020

死海
Dead Sea

this is your street   this is your accent
this is your flesh   minced meat
a dead sea to stuff a bun
your own stink made to order

a pasta wrapper radiantly flattens the sea's surface
rolled flat again and again   Harvest Home[1] needs no fancy edging
dead bats   rabbits   deer   expose small white bones
inform on running   inform on breathing

sense of smell   informs on molecule rallies flying through the sky
lungs   inform on hidden blood-red data
on TV a fat face carved in relief slowly stammers every word
reads out informers in single file turning into faces patched with masks

steam's fancy edging chases newly open bamboo steamers
charred-smelling fancy edging rises from disciplined haircuts
dead fishies[2] drift with the tide   with no high hopes of escaping underwater
there is no underwater in your world

all that is left is bare   denuded salt
scorching rocky spindrift inside you
every morning   changing channels of filth from far and near
switching off the heart   that fish bone

---

1. *Qingfeng* (Celebrating Harvest) is a popular shop in Beijing's Qianmen Street, famously visited by President Xi Jinping to show how close he is to the masses. The shop sells *baozi*, the Chinese ravioli, which are often served in soup, and much of the imagery in this poem derives from *baozi*. [BH]
    2. The poet uses an unorthodox plural, as do I. [BH]

this is your glory   a spittle-drenched paper sealing strip
aid-built fancy edgings on all the empty cities
a sea slows down along with you   gets old   blinded
nothing has changed   this place   life is not exceptional

it's a sin   undiscardable punishment banquets
holding flat a vision of a bowl of bitterly salt rippling
your real name manufactures tears   every drop
holds high official authentication from the Motherland

a ball of exploding sunlight splashes in the depths of a fat face
keeps rationing forever locked up DNA
wraps up tight   gulps down   the funeral urns' generous affection
a colossal virus whispers intimately in your ear

28 January 2020

青草祭

Green Grass Offering

(for Deng Shiping)[3]

there's a kind of delicate children's feet that hibernate
there's a kind of green   like a gently swinging stone wall
moved underground as soon as water gushes   hogtied leaves
are hogtying children   running between springtime and springtime

that human face that seeps from grass tips   trampled ten thousand times
growing ten thousand times   heavy rain buried sixteen years ago
with a corpse   holding its breath it goes on to swell
the sportsground is a wild unrelocatable grave

a human-shaped void   windows see the unseeable
words of names   read   a taboo lesson texts block
he should go back   stumble either side of sixteen years
his death   the dying can't die

then green grass has grown   green grass grows year after year
a lawn   lake of green   packed with ritual newly started school
green grass   carrying his drinking-straw lunch
sits among the children   restores the stench of decay   the taste of
    unavenged ghosts

he weeps   sobs choke the soil
bulldozers flatten Earth   a pit of shame
no need to be deeper   furrily wipe the horizon   spread
hugely small massacres   tinily huge massacres

---

3. Deng Shiping, originally from Huaihua in Hunan Province, was a teacher at
Xinhuang No. 1 High School in charge of technical supervision of the school sports
ground during construction. Because he refused to sign off on shoddy building
work for the headmaster's relatives, he disappeared on 22 January 2003; his bones
were found four metres under the school sports ground, hogtied, his hands behind
his back. [YL]

there's a kind of delicate   takes children
locks them night and day in tombs
there's a kind of green raises fences   time that no one believes in
looking outwards with no expectation

虚构·2020
Fiction 2020
(for Geling)

Nabokov carrying his butterflies   drills out
the reflection of the big lake   hey!   who are you?   a tiny
fox spirit   a curve of white snake   at the same time you're a handsome
     young scholar
in love with written fate and reborn there on the quiet
mentions a plague city   then can't trek out of faint whimpers
lie down to hear   the bone-crushing rattle in the music
who says they're coming back?   Hell spurts from a shred of the great river
grips your throat   waves kick you like lovesickness
hometown ghost stories eternally murmur of this staying away

people tacitly accept the fiction   as bamboo leaves in your yard
wake early too   whirl   transformed into the white page of first light
in every word light dancer's steps   though the stage is still empty
the original of emptiness   holding in Father's cough   a poem
crammed with the absence of departed souls   like lost manuscripts
using the dark to be lost again and again   forbidden breath roosts in
forbidden filming   an unbegun metaphor
stares at a vast emptiness of flesh and blood   Father drips back into the shingle
another role waits for disappointed beauty

is it you?   an ancient melancholy now deep enough
to choke time to death   a donated youth sighs and performs
both are true   2020 squeezes into the thinnest cocoon
squirms   swells splits   opens butterfly wings bright as Hell
Nabokov is here   Father is here   great History
ghosts impossible to wash out   smile and dream   only one drop
who reads and understands is heartbroken as the words   inside and outside
     the window
the same touch of moon shadow   bamboo leaves sough and vacate music
the first lamp leads countless shadows swirling out of a body

26 September 2020, Berlin

魇·2020
Nightmares 2020

1

who does a poem cry for help to?   as you cower
foul stench   supported by the cellar walls
a universe of breeding cockroaches
rub their dream claws   sawdust fills the air

wood's bad words   throw away the shape of a year
wood   now so tame it can rot into any jail term

skulls   workshops of bad dreams
gasps   manufacture analgesic ritual
lives   tiny tiny hush-money

can't be seen   can't be paid up
staring at neon screens   you smile greasier still
perfectly fit to be murdered

2

shutting a poetess in a dungeon is a kind of pleasure
hearing a chisel gouge through a convict carpenter's hand
is a kind of pleasure

strip clothes off right down to the flesh
strip flesh off right down to the stink that knows
neither you nor me   wail   even more stinking

2020 is a cliff   oh jump   dummies

this excruciatingly slow shattering seems familiar
spring flowers and autumn moons shackled here too   reciting
the knowledge of false reincarnations   shouldering blood's viscosity
like a poem no one has read   in the gale of History
there has only ever been pitch-black   walking alone

3

reality's filthy fat hands   drill through
your keel   cold cold image of seawater pouring in
concrete as a chair   you obediently sit down
tell lies   this is how a lifetime of waiting goes by

watch the jungle where voters break bones on TV
indifferent   another day to exchange gang-rape tickets
indifferent   nailed on the end of a fishbone
confess   a lifetime of being depraved has no end

the language of mockery flooded to the nostrils   it remembers
how lingering choking to death is   a string of bad news bubbles
sneaks back to your mouth   shaped like a micro-Hell
a locked-in lifetime scrapped long ago

4

2020   a virus is not a nightmare   bearing the pain is
smashing is not a nightmare   unified deaf-muteness of the shatters is

there's a kind of poison that daily elevates your unpoisonable nature

there's a kind of eternal positivity wants at all costs to cough up
a never-unblocked heart   a natural enemy carrier clatters
you must wake   sample the flavour of sinking in nightmares

that perfect craftsmanship   picks up with its fingers
each and every crushed flower carving   reversing
bursts into bloom   reverts to the neck-snapping instant
the abyss is so tender   there is no abyss at all

'Master   I am drop of water beside you'[4]
the most shameless drop

---

4. The title of one of my poems made as an offering to the poet Qu Yuan
(*c.* 340-278 BCE). [YL]

5

everyone is a catastrophic pandemic
your rotten tree trunk   my rotten tree trunk   drifted so far
run aground this far   zero meaning has ripped down 2020
a seamless jail term unworthy of Doomsday   has spat out 2020
the verdict   one thin page   to live is to dance in the square
to suffer is to dance in the square   you must go on   give up the appeal
filth pricked out by a needle piles up in the eye   in the heart
execution pursues footsteps   larger than terror   smaller than curses
rotting History in this moment   this moment demands
life from everyone   who says the Chairman's rostrum isn't a Bridge of
    No Return?
quietly trampling a poem is a limitless pleasure
as it is crammed into the coffin   completing your howling dreamland

19th October—25th November 2020

瘟疫实验室（一—三）
Plague Laboratory (1-3)

1

blue bottles are rinsed once each morning
little white mice yawn   rub their eyes   lick their claws
fattened   their breath gleams   a holidaying sky
bird wings   wipe the dirt off aeroplanes inch by inch

one beautiful side of death
never unplugged   an indeterminate charm boiling beside you

weep and wail enough   then you'll see tears are the feeblest of molluscs
body temperature sensors scan distorting mirrors
nothing to do with the abyss   the ration of death is in the formula
long ago weightless   who   flapping antiseptic wings
dances and flies   what ritual isn't overtaking the ritual of the vacuum?

a pandemic is like happiness   it comes and goes in a rush
surrounds the farewells of snow-white dummies   in anticipation brakes
        the aftertaste

just testing   whether the black boiling water of this pandemic
has splashed into the ants' nest before?   memory
caresses sleek seductive flesh   with how many volatile zeroes?
one micro-instant   your fine downy hairs lightly flick
the libation cup   echoes of shouts are nothing
a clean container   its disposability disappoints ruin and beauty

grief is so null and void   it drops out of red-letter days
swinging long sleeves   amazed it can still be smashed to pieces

2

we split open thorax after thorax
what can we be hunting out?
a slice of white coral lung   vastness that can't be coughed up in a
    thousand years

implanted in lattice narrower than a cellule
implied eyeballs staring at their origin
bat Zero   flitted through a dusk all hung with little faces

all sickening   in love with saturating a chemical-tasting moonlight

yet the blood-dripping cave doesn't know it's sick from the top down
and the tide advances   advances   rippling around toes
as if we are forever walking straight   as if diameter isn't illusion
stewing down this moment   pushing and shoving in the flag-raising room
departed souls stand outside the window   pay no heed to two fleshy
    wings blindly flapping

history   only one big blunder   gathering the white of white coral

the black of black years   strangles unmoving directions
nothing but bad news   one squeaking swoop
dismantles all directions   bats seem to laugh seem to weep   zero
counterpoint to endless waves emptily rising and falling in the same place
sipping internal secretions   each lung advertising its own suffocation
each reflection vertically sliced by the other's
glass curtain wall   on the flame of a silent eternally-burning lamp
our destinies have slowly boiled dry

the pot bottom laid bare   the swallows' ban begins to soar again

3

lyric poetry is not enough   though love
has nowhere to retreat to   poetry pitch-black as karma

a lake   opens a bright fresh mouth
that holds a little poplar thermometer   greenness thickens again
a false abyss   in closely fondled silence
a swirl of words hug and kiss a swirl of time passing
yet time passing   endlessly defaults on a name

we grow old   never old enough
we're young   never young enough

the lake waits here   a swaying crystallised stone
waits until footsteps   slow   stumble   lean in to shadow
a sigh just shaped from a thousand years before
slips down   yours or mine?   outer space crowded with sitters
explodes like first love   saturates   hears how alike human lives are

never grieve or look back again   then a poem is crystallised
cold and bright fingertips   strip off
the bitter astringency of ancient lotus seed hearts
underwater is awake   independent of talent   independent of miracle
history without hope

fluctuates between small plagues
everyone must be old once   fully ripen once   sit down
be rocked a while by their own tiny time immemorial
more than lake   more than sea   ancient lotus seeds
secretly live and love with mud   poetry steadily implants what's foredoomed

discloses drowned cries for help

一只名叫"希望"的瓮
An Urn Called 'Hope'

evil presses down   day and daily we sink into a handful of ash
borrow each other's phosphorescence to identify   yet another shattering
is the same shattering   behind us a cold rough container
waits here   nestles in   sucks at doom

     a pulped life filled in with a word: hope

tonight   the sky is an urn   held
by echoes   a hand that presses an upended key   reverse reflection of
light in amber   me   a mantis staring at itself
fangs bared and claws shown   a gleaming doomsday

     full decay lights up an empty word: hope

a flesh and blood funnel   nothing has changed
funnel of gurgling water   twirling deep pitch-black sighs
tongues go downstream   an endless chain of ash mountains choked speechless
a shard of dry bone scrapes names away   the kind of deathly pale no one ever
     lived in

     an empty foot violently kicking an iron door: hope

I fear the light   I'm turning into light   a mantis
stays where it is for a million years   greenness   freezes
dreams of escape   my aliveness carves my non-existence
amber hugs   a day of dying for real can't not exist

     flooding a lifelong persisting falsity: hope

the loneliest word   secretes plurality
one goes missing once   empty books for all of us
burned and hidden   the cinerary urn drinks all the bitter wine up
phosphorescence glitters on the lips   sticks to spilt curses

     complete and perfect as depravity: hope

奥威尔的新年
Orwellian New Year

1

I am Smith   turning my diary to the next page
what can I still write?   Julia's waist has melted into twilight
sunshine's scarlet belt tighter and tighter
our sex tightened down to freezing point   all the way from 1984
hardens   touches the April 4th crusted every day on our backs
from Julia's young flesh shoots a look
nailed into withered betrayal   as the betrayal practiced on a mother
a face is that hole   where all memories for burning can be flung
blowing away her hyacinth hairline as she sits up
dazzling blue   casts off slenderer birdsong
I am Smith   a page of twilight paper   written on
2019 still hasn't totally blackened   Julia's weariness in bed
like an ever-unrepayable loan   stared at again   her flesh buds
London's packed pubs are an underground watercourse
as if fictional love fictionalises the lover
and overhead the never switched off moonlight   a mannequin in the mirror
walks closer   catches up with a cage   my Julia
don't dodge the pack of squealing   little beasts frantic to be at it
rats' teeth leaping from the paper   this time   even biting is empty

2

I am Julia   no one betrays me
as the *I love you* dustbin is overturned again
I'm rushing through the grey mist of every year
always a gaze shooting me in the back   knocking me in
after my death   a pretty slogan will automatically update
1984's sex appeal rubs against 2019's men
the viscera of time diverting that pond   lawn   elm woods
make him shoot himself empty as a rabbit   so embracing the species
sleep a while   every dream will enhance the quality of the torture
every landscape painting will refresh the eyes in ambush
every orgasm splash out a yell   link them up in a chain

little sweetie   oh come here   treading on the second hand of New Year
a snow-white breast like a ball of mud under the black police boots
(how often has that same short video been broadcast?)
youth's film script crashes into my arms   blind trundling flesh
make the passion for resistance or destruction identical
even I have not betrayed myself   I have only
come back   a waxy yellow face   always stripped bare
when I'm pulled out again and again upside down   I recognise
the pool of clotted blood   and the world

3

I am Orwell   my Minitrue
sentences you all to love a skeleton with hands tied behind its back
rotted grass on a sports ground blowing a whistle
the wooden bed above the junk shop next door groaning night and day
children goose-step   through the soaked scaffolding
sticky street under your feet   time's viscosity of nothingness
can't tear you off one from another   can only contaminate you all
on the window glass the darkest school grows
raindrops' Braille   a sunken ship pulls sister's drowning
great steadily blurring eyes in the deep sea   overlook
another night sky that filtered New Year fireworks
I am Orwell   a book has required all destinies of now
Smith roosts in the treetops   hands himself over to the white of the gale
        white of words
Julia splatters like a tiny coral   throws out
the paperweight of life   useless beauty is fragile as this
the rutting season of your ruin   turn it again and it's only a single thin
        page again
this wall of the worst news builds inside you   everyone hiding in a bunker
cheering   Room 101 is safest   warmest
like a borderless grammatical particle   bracing beautifully decorated bars
red-hot curling steel rampantly generates from terror
a precision-guided   heat-tempered heart
bombs me   strengthens me   endlessly returning to ritual
tongue-fur's vast collapse reports to its source:
'Your hot main course is here, Mr Orwell.'

奥维德的泉水
Ovid's Spring Water

the Black Sea turbulent by my side   as I walk on the square
to pass under your bronze brow   an empty bottle in my hand
the September sun approaches from behind   waits to come closer
a stone trough carves into a mouth-shape   hears an accent
jangle and tinkle   that boat still doesn't know where it should sail to
on the mountain that olive-green stone stair has been worn smooth
I bring the whole world's thirst   in exchange for a drop of your cool
loneliness   always like newly-wrung hill wind   sea breeze
Sulmona[5] embedded in the seashore   hears leaky footsteps
leak into my body   Ovid   where are you?

we all can change   like these words pressed under the paperweight
of the ocean   written scroll by scroll into the void
a marble stone from ancient Rome   holds up the exotic smell of mint
by the wings of my nose   metamorphosing gods metamorphose into a poem
when a rotten dinghy upended by the Black Sea is most pornographic
it sinks fully loaded with girls   azure stone smashes infant babbling
a street called Ovid has never gone to sea
yet has voyaged farthest   'I grew up drinking this spring water'
in the bottle   the water level of glittering channel shards rises
seeking to drown some unknown voice   'No one knows me'

two thousand years   one exile   the sound of water being born
sip the dying's water sound   waves polish two statues
two reflections a thousand miles apart pull an endless road straight
let a Black Sea seep into my throat   let you walk beside me
so alive   spring water opens the most ancient book
Ovid   you are empty   arriving at your new strange land
then pouring us full of distance   a little town like a footnote
under a rose-pink sky with the word *leave* written on it
changing the changes of babbling water   we have all come back
have died countless times   are filtered incomparably pure

---

5. Ovid's birthplace, in Abruzzo, Italy. [BH]

落: 肖像
Falling: A Portrait

the valley's red mist is also an endless verb
boughs engrave your fresh clarity
like a still life   down-turned in a split second

an astringently blushing face
detained in the light   space is waiting
one light sound about to be bared

one 'aah'   clearly hears its own originality
at the destination   one poem's vivid form
has grown into a dancer's tripping moves

this moment   wildfires of tender April green
live inside you   August's casement crashes open
her smile   pierces your insides

blade polished silver-bright   cuts silver-bright autumn clouds
the valley revolves   because you leap out of the sky
because falling is a kind of thought

a hill path hidden in frosty pink brushstrokes
dives down   deck and notes of music sink into cold light
push away without end the Mother Earth inside you

to mimic a theme of the moon   theme of the night
face   enduring the hands of love
converts that caress

still life   when was it ever still?
in the hills   watch a red leaf bedecking a rosy cheek
watch fiery connotation gush forth

a fate quietly changed
from this moment on
you're not called a poet   you *write poems*

16 November 2010—21 February 2011

2019年12月19日: 冬至和诗
19th December 2019: A Response Poem on the Winter Solstice

(for Andreas, Ines and Cornelie von Bismarck)

'form or content?'
only hear once quietened down   the dark is their entirety
a fir tree's days spread underfoot soon or late
a clutch of words whitened on paper ash   revised into a sort of coldness
sodden mud is dodging poetry   is stuck tight to poetry
what we've read up to today is more than every day

'the problem of meaning'
we from our direction   you from yours
converge into the longest night   fir branches set off by small white flowers
sparkles   the candle flame in the glass still like
the lamp on your desk   below the old stone wall of your grandfather's grave
kindles a little random hip-hop doggerel in your eyes

'you don't know or can't decide'
now   a bunch of shy   smiling gazes
endlessly lift   up clip pine needles that drop water
and our long overdue late arrival   but there's no blame
you write down the flesh and blood possessing you   sky's grey elegance
love's unburdening   still struggling to take root

'and must not envy anyone else'
our recital is buried in your soliloquy
this little gravel path reaches the forest edge   your edge
who knew a heart had quietly wept for so long?
time's axis   screwed tight from every direction
the deep pit of a human form forever unfillable

'this is not this decision: elegance or wildness'
there are never two days   escape again from forty years old
and only escape into one day   like an impaled bone spur
binding   the little winter book that death retells

37

carried with you at all times   carried with us at all times
between pitch-black branches   silvery white but certainly not lake water

                            'they must combine to be true beauty!'
there is a bird standing up there   it astonishes a creature of tears
there are vast immensities told by the dark   ineffable immensities
long ago stored in the faces of unreachable children
seep into us   birdsong loses count of the wreckage
who knows a history that kidnaps our kin one by one?

                                    'beauty is not naturally born'
it conceives of poetry   it matures like poetry
you inhabit us   mother guard oh the candle flame like candle flame
guard oh the darkness   the long line of the horizon knows no word of
        farewell
the long verse of the horizon delineates the meaning of farewell
damp black   most perfect black   must nowhere bid a last farewell

                        'but make no mistake, wickedness is fleeting'
in a tiny cemetery   a clutch of paper ash remains on the fir branches
a son's whitening words left on fir branches
a new home   raises each similar homecoming step
only hear once quietened down
a crane begins to call in a boundless heart[6]

---

6. Italicised lines translated from Andreas von Bismarck's German to Chinese
by Yang Lian [BH]:
Form oder Inhalt?
Die Frage nach dem Sinn halt!
Weißt Du es nicht oder kannst Dich nicht entscheiden,
musst nicht denken, die and'ren haben 'nen Plan und niemanden beneiden.
Es geht nicht um die Entscheidung: Eleganz oder Wildheit,
denn nur zusammen is es echte Schönheit!
Schönheit ist nicht selbstverständlich,
aber sei Dir gewiss, Bosheit ist nicht vergänglich!

柏林安哈尔特火车站大门
Berlin Anhalter Bahnhof Main Gate[7]

the China roses bloom hugely red and shameless   the gravel path
leads to the platform in the photo   metres deep under my feet
they queued up to move   dawdling towards the lonely arched entranceway
Berlin Anhalter Bahnhof had nothing to do with destinations
it is its own destination   an ornately-carved tombstone
standing in sunset shadows   an openwork eye-socket
dragging a green football field   1942 comes wildly running
2020 sits all around the terraces   the China rose axletrees rumbling
trundle   flesh and blood of the dead has donated a line of numbers
in city and cemetery   the 1942 wind busily blowing
2020's azure glowers vacantly at time
the rail track's assembly line invisibly tightens a little one-year-old face
a little embraced passenger   looking up at the one-line resumé
on the brass plaque   sucking identical ruin in both sides of the gates
this locomotive   only passes ruin between departure and arrival
below the tropical plants carved in brick   three wide open oven doors
spit flame   smell of tightly-packed humans never alights from the train
landscape of ash set in a constantly-changing frame   parallel
spread-out shadows   my setting sun lies down in someone unknown's
    setting sun
hears an artillery shell just passed through   unstitch a weird blossom of steel

        that statue sitting all by itself
overlooks a deep pit   where snow-white flesh was tumbled and heaped
fingerprints left on skin   and dust have signed girlish charms
and putrefaction   the delineated seabed fragile as plaster
dismal as bronze   soft limbs breasts   genitals

---

7. Between 1942 and 1945, Anhalter Bahnhof was the station from which trains transported Jewish people to the concentration camps. All that survives of it now is the main entrance. [YL]

amid a waterfall   moulded into the first draft of a China rose
huge down-dripping billows held up on one hand
sinks down to   every day's   today's Gates of Hell
at the end of the gravel path   Anhalter Bahnhof heavy as ghosts
we queued up to move   shadows covered in just-chiselled stone chips
flowers like convicts with pierced collarbones led back to full bloom
the statue's empty eye sockets filled with poems of non-existence
how many more deaths must there be before the word History has had
     enough?
the Gates of Hell's other side is here   an idea that will never heal
adorns me like a composition that will never be completed   above and
     below ground
overlook each other   2020 mute and helpless
poured into 1942   like a gouged-out memory
the deep pit of humans still waits for its blackest moment
those never-arriving   log past stones   add
a whistle   fragments everywhere stiff and bright as new

16 August—26 November 2020

40

树林中的铁轨
Railway Tracks in the Woods

white birches rise lithe and limber as curling smoke
green speeding up   to chase the broken tracks

the dotted line of an explosion   leading the dancing girl's moves
drills deeper down every day

flames of war climb quietly out of rust like dead snakeskin
whirling shrapnel carefully counts the unfinished trains

with one jump kids on skateboards   lightly held
waistlines   squash into tightly screwed-in leaves

a poem of rotting rail sleepers   exposes Sunday's
rivets   groaning under the heavy pressure of human nature

charming rebound for the dead   map of an underground hub
like stones   or bones fallen out of a body

preserving the parallel   who can't see   is on the train
non-stop to Siberia's tenderest snow and ice

white birch woods gallop   the signal towers' pitch-black windows
staring at another bunch of newly green rumbling wheels and axles

the chemical taste of the picnic   the chemical taste of the lovemaking
have unwearyingly scrubbed the wall graffiti-covered again

tree roots and the loveliest white bones
covertly clench the urge to apply the brakes

the terminus is motionless   half the track passes by whistling
springtime fresh and new as reverse speed

so   tell me   what is thrown aside
the world or this poem of pain?

24 August—25 November 2020

音乐会上的狐狸幽灵
Phantom Foxes at a Concert[8]

the room is a grove   how many lives of the cello
squeeze in the window   bluer still   foxes
walk   brush close to everyone   pass through everyone
turn into a heard   trembling under the fingers   world
that is a gigantic wound

melodies   played once then reincarnated once
like a far-off shadow jumping a hedge in one bound
twitching little noses   smelling the empty den of notes
and lying languidly in a purple flower bed where a noble son lingers
glancing round once   to stare at another previous lifetime

C-minor   hand in hand little brother composer leads
the piano's soft sigh   D-minor   big sister is quietly weeping
charming twinned deaths summon dogs' barking far and near
what ripples in the heart   is still sobbing no matter how lovely
foxes   overspill out of the body little by little

pitch and yaw like a violin   language darkening and also brightening
those sharp ears   clever faces   slim waists curling up like smoke
made by fate   heard and knew the taste of temptation
tiptoeing   (or motionless)   have forded flames
a poem of fascination has no need for obscurity

---

8. This poem is about a family of foxes that lived in Cornelie von Bismarck's garden. Cornelie would feed them, and they would come closer and closer to humans, even stayed just outside the door when she held a family concert in the house. But the neighbours weren't happy with the foxes: in the end, they caught them and sent them who knows where – the foxes disappeared. This poem tries to imagine their souls are still with us, having even become music and poetry, and in this way it tries to bring the foxes back.

C-minor and D-minor are the keys of brother and sister Felix and Fanny Mendelssohn's Piano Trios. [YL]

this is the foxes' moment   thin thin calls
ear-splitting   when they escape into where escape's impossible
a silhouette imbued with love picks up children in its mouth
stops on a dirge-woven green lawn
we curl up long handsome tails   sitting there

羽毛·石头

Feather – Stone

(for Elisabeth Biron Von Curland)

the lake is a likeness
on your hand   this living goose quill pen
has shattered silence   a far-flying wild geese skein

like a string of inkblots splashing out of an old Chinese verse
a tiny black pebble is chasing those wingtips
imagine   who is running away on the cloud canvas?

you   or the lake   with goose-quill oars move a face
water's sound immersed in a wild goose's thirty-five round trips
do they equal three thousand five hundred?   a palette of distant hill-space

quietly changes every instant into the beauty that is changeless
the stone kept by your window   the candle on the table
fly   through rebirth of deep-embosomed departed souls of darkness

along snow-white engraved marbling   this deportation
gathers the weight of stones   the feather's lightness
overflows from a newly-completed work of art   this isolation

incomparably ardent   almost perfuming   in the wind life sways
a mass of seething waves that smashed and broke the shore
ripple a face   projection of every face

your brush point   dripping the colours of hills   colours of sky
a self-portrait shining with glistening blots
reflecting the world   loving it and leaving it to its endless drifting by

11 August 2019

石头·羽毛

Stone – Feather

(for Christiana Buron)

Dante's terza rima
holding her hands to teach a daughter to collage a hell
stone steps lead down one by one   extermination's formula

thin as a paper of epidermis
a skull's mother of pearl   a dead fish horizon
shredded rhythms bite down on glued-up rhythms

the darkness   only seen with eyes closing
decays into a baby   the wire netting brakes the ocean waves
hands stretching from the volcano's mouth   gently brush the strings

death lays bare a butterfly   inset in the eye socket
it's reality   the roar of Bosnian guns is too close
children kneeling   tiny breasts   slurry-saturated

in the feather's vacuum tubes mothers are hiding
tears falling is milk flowing   one drop of beauty secreted in the body
making you suck   the blackest bit of human living

disaster's steps lead down one by one   how deep can they still go?
snare for humans   snare for words   each step entering the now
never reaching the seabed   everywhere stuck in the seabed below

terror's blueprint   only one page
already written poem of flesh and blood   poem of stone
a weightless feather has summed up a future age

13 September 2019

"金沙，请听二十秒钟雨声"
'Jinsha, please listen to 20 seconds of rain'
(for Jigen and Wang Fang)

'Jinsha,[9] please listen to 20 seconds of rain'
Jigen who doesn't write poetry   pushes our hearts

                                                        into poetry

at Jinsha this minute   heavy rain
pours endlessly into a coal-black container

twenty seconds   a nation collapsed into
another nation   Sika deer cross a water forest
look back   stare with round bronze eyes
elapsed implication never leaking from the archaeological grid

twenty seconds   twenty historical foreign tongues
gurgle as splashing water   all our poems
gushing from the eaves   trickle into a poem of darkness

the sound of rain brooks no dispute   it identifies
an invisible lake   we don't recognise Du Fu[10]
Du Fu doesn't recognise the figure on a ladder of jade *cong* tubes[11]
shinning up five thousand years

gold mask covers inverted on the same black hole-like face
oh listen   stranger   next to this shower of rain
how much black time have we caught?

---

9. Jinsha is an archaeological site in Chengdu, Sichuan Province. Jinsha culture (1200-650 BCE). [BH]

10. Du Fu (712-770 CE), is regarded as perhaps the greatest of all Chinese poets. [BH]

11. 琮 *cong* (pron. *tsoong*) are prehistoric artefacts of unknown function, tubes with a square outer section and a circular inner section. They appear from the Neolithic onward, mostly in jade or pottery. [BH]

how much more must we still catch?
black   this night swallowed by Jinsha's open-mouthed
sediment to our breastbones   tailbones   an intaglio line
long enough   ancient enough   welcoming the desiccation of death
ends at the bottom of a pit that could never be deeper

this infinitely large house   can only await the next dig[12]

---

12. Tang Jigen and Wang Fang are well-known archaeologists: Tang is a Shang Dynasty (*c*.1600–1046 BCE) specialist, and is leader of the Henan Yin Ruins Archaeological Team. Wang is a specialist in jades from high antiquity, and is deputy director of the Jinsha Site Museum. In May 2019, when torrential rain fell during an evening of poetry and archaeology there, Jigen asked us to listen to the rain for twenty seconds. And that was how this poem came to be. [YL]

在上博撫摸一只西周編钟

Touching a Set of Western Zhou Dynasty Bells
in Shanghai Museum
(for Zhou Ya)

dark green skin like a little lake   to have stroked it
is a fit of shivering   water surface has broken
unfading and unfalling flowers underwater   expose
the accent of the dead   but don't recall their death
cooling residual warmth oozes into the clan register   the more it's touched
the further it gets   two millennia squeezed tight into you dug out
in the deep well of a chest cavity   darkness salvages
a forgery of darkness   your growth was always a skeleton
your surname has silted up with mud still suspended at
the height of the carvings   hear the picked-out heartbeat
beating again and again regardless of inside or out
history   from void to void   there is nothing can be lost

a hypothetical hum doesn't know who speaks
where speaks   words are one frequency   hand
another   the same melancholy intonation
calibrates you and me   organs waiting two millennia for meaning
put on beast masks   each becomes the other's oblation
what came through the times other than terror is still terror
palm stuck close to the container   feels unavenged ghosts resonate
what came through the grave other than tinnitus is still tinnitus
this hole is unfillable   this time of downward
climbing   holds edges and corners   holds scars
a dark green breeze buried by the side of convulsions
the lift comes on down   we are deathly silence reforged

听溥雪斋弹《梅花三弄》

Listening to Pu Xuezhai Playing *Three Plum Blossom Airs*

whether or not   great rivers and seas are lighter than one plum blossom petal
whether or not   plum   blooms like a music score   floats down like a music
   score

when exquisite beauty   is unseen   when scent can't be smelled
hear   your garden   my garden

a sinuous cloister   winds around stone   winds around bamboo
winds around your brush   smashes   scatters and fells spotless white specks
   from the sky

who runs away from home   must keep on running away from home
who there is nowhere to bury   can only hide in a broken string

so much despair needed   before ruin can be vested in a whiff of fragrance
hear   a ghost yourself   let ghosts play on to their hearts' content

whether or not   the stamen long ago knew if damp viscera were fresh or rotten
all strung up for a beating   faraway pain hiding everywhere

making you   making me   leave words outside the door
so naked the sense of hearing   so chance-met the sense of hearing

August 30th 1966   a never-imagined sweltering summer heat
forced you into the cold night   you walked alone with your little daughter

and fled   a cold withered landscape as far as the eye could see
in the dead angle of terror   who isn't Ni Zan?   who isn't Xu Wei?[13]

---

13. Ni Zan (1301-1374) and Xu Wei (1521-1593, pron. *shü way*) were both
notable Chinese painters. [BH]

who wasn't buried in the vast snowstorm of your name
hear   plum blossom waits in the direction of disappearance

2019   the zither's sound unchanging   its ceasing unchanging
whether or not   you know I might be born in your sighs

whether or not   the scented dropping-away skeleton between the notes
flutters up just so   garden and graveyard both blown away by the wind[14]

---

14. Pu Xuezhai (pron. *Shü-eh zhai*) was a member of the Qing Dynasty's royal family, the son of a Manchu prince; his birth name was Aisin-Gioro Pujin, but he took the style-name of Xuezhai [meaning *Snow Studio* – BH] and became generally known by that name. He was a well-known as a painter, and was also a virtuoso of the *guqin* 古琴 (pron. *goo-chin*), the Chinese horizontal harp: like his painting, his playing has a timeless appeal, a pure beauty, and great elegance. He was born on 30 August 1893, and in 1966 he came up against the terror of the Cultural Revolution. In August of that year (some say on the 30th, his birthday) he disappeared with his daughter the Sixth Princess, to a destination unknown. One of his former homes was at what was once 25, West Hall Lane Xitangzi, Wangfujing, in central Beijing. He later sold it to my great-grandfather Liu Xiezhi. Its courtyard was of marble, exquisite, yet snug and comfortable, and is said to have been designed by Pu himself. So, it happened that I was listening to a recording of Pu Xuezhai playing *Three Plum Blossom Airs*, and it brought to mind all he lived through, which gave me the notion of attempting a poem in praise of him. [YL]

溆浦美人夜歌
Xupu Beauty Nocturne[15]

they are all waiting elsewhere   but all you want is night
all you want is a river   a railing looking out over pitch-black water
holding up that waist   under the cliff the Master is coming for you
the water-murmuring shore in an appointment   bridge   lamplight
dummied a thousand years   the dark's passion lifting bright beautiful flesh
where is Xupu?   beauty's curse is forever endless
walk on water   never lacking the poet's far sight next time
a river also holds up two lovesick organs on their way
stand in night   who isn't naked lifelong   hanging lonely?
mumbling drenches every empty hollow   crease   passage
stamen firmly hooked   all you want is this nothingness

they are all waiting elsewhere   a room is breeding
foxes   a perfume-rank bed widens the riverbed
flushed spring colours of peach blossom saved a thousand years on your body
always kept here   opens two leaves of a small muddy shore
the Master comes by moonlight   well knows how to pursue the gaps in
    humans
wants a bamboo shoot tip exposed a midnight   peeled a thousand years
it's still tender   wants a tiny mouth to bend down and play with the
    hasty sound of water
to call anyone's name is like forging   the fox's dazzle
belly a snow-white glimmer   riding the Dark Creator
swaying   your sucked-dry look is like a world that couldn't care less
ruined   nowhere to run   Xupu is too far away

---

15. Xupu County is in Hunan Province (pronounced *shüpoo*, the first syllable
rhyming with French tu). It is the place most often mentioned in the poetry
attributed to Qu Yuan (*c.*340-278BCE), China's first named poet (pronounced *chü
yüan*). It was then a remote part of the Kingdom of Chu, to which Qu Yuan was
banished, but according to legend, he committed suicide by drowning himself in
the Miluo River, while only halfway there.

they are all waiting elsewhere   the great river of a poem
passing as in spate   breathes gently if it wants to breathe gently   wants
      a tiger growl
so distant hills lie down beside you   softly bite you
play hard with you   a fatal void that will not bypass flesh
words can't fill up   only a long night will do   indulged in once
the Master can't come back now   incense's name reaches bone-marrow
doesn't see humans   every idea towers upwards   soul or ghost
tonight in an intangible home   wanting   that fissure of Xupu
thinking of extreme endlessly continuing cracking open
water spurts out   the railing right beside the spray and splatter
Master   only the blackest womb is fit to store this howling wind and rain

23 January 2020

星期一，以西湖为背景
Monday, with West Lake for a Backdrop

that day   the museum   where Madam White Snake and Little Su are migrant
      workers
is closed   our boat sails between poems' lotus leaves
seeking Little Green Snake   sunshine   wave shadows' slow upward curl
steps into May   there must be a big bloom by your face
scent   changing and changeless   snake tongues lick the boat's hull
spit out a shore with a pagoda lonely playing at being a tombstone
        that day   beauty was our theme
        beauty   stripped right down only a drop of water so muddy

lonely as West Lake   buried in a history with splashing oars
and buried by the row of high-rises behind   we are down a hole
hanging round   a century stinking of gore
always making eyeglasses wetter   father's skyline
gradually farther and deeper   guarding the window by the desk   you
day after day of far sight grown into a poem of spreading states of mind
        West Lake's every soft sigh   rhyming with life
        endless Broken Bridges on green waves   every jade dripping and bloody

speeches hatch into butterflies   and under the brush a painting confirms
that ghost of beauty   like a prodigal climbing the boat's hull   sparkly
grabs at you   waking with difficulty each morning   this destiny
is not misfortune   the next transformation tolerates us with stabbing agony
plan   two fish swimming into a girlfriend's version of the text
the poetics of chance meeting   stretched a little to set off lake and hills
        needles of speeches   suture up unseen
        the cloudless sky embraces you and me with a heart beating faintly

an exquisite book infinitely large   infinitely sore
equal to a definition of love   that day   the silence we crossed
so brutal at the same time   no need to listen to the deepest bass
only ought to think   a sacrifice glancing sidelong at the vista
swallowses fly bravely from birth   into death   in your pretty glance

doubly wander   thousand-year solitude incomparably heavy   incomparably
    light
        an exquisite book   restored again and again
        us at the origin   every trace exuding Little Green Snake's beauty

6 August 2019

邋遢大士九十歌

Messmaster 90 Song[16]

(for my big bro Guanguan)

mess mess   messy-mess   the Master takes Heiya by the hand[17]
sings a happy 90 song   smiles and plants birthday flowers
come on   hard times shed one by one   the land whimsically disrobed
it comes   ocean an opera party   white clouds like hemp and mulberry
your battledress nakedly revealing a few horizons
plus a 20-year-old village accent   cannon fire still not familiar with this
    world
nowhere promoted like a poem   pillowed on the straits
listen   your old mum's warnings   that PIN number buried in the yellow
    earth
indecipherable   then a lifetime washed in the spring sun's chill
90-year-old   with 70 years jumping off a cliff
realising as you jump   the sound of wind beside you   sound of rain
    sound of tides
all joined up to poetry's National Army   the youngest squaddies the
    most genteel
girl bullseye   only waiting for a sharpshooter to pull the trigger
youth nothing to do with age   a painting swings its long hair
always upping the strength of the blast   every word has its posture   its
    aria
a little carrying-pole   a stage chasing you   wherever you go
wherever you're free-spirited   life's theatre needs no sages   C-in-Cs

---

16. Guanguan, a Taiwan poet of the older generation, has a studio named Messy
Studio. I love my big bro Guanguan for the indomitable free spirit in his poetry
and his person, and admire him even more for being one of that generation who
survived the hurricane of History and had the great virtue of inheriting and passing
on the ancestral flame of Chinese-language poetry. In 2019, just at the time of his
birthday, I made a deliberate attempt to copy his style of recitation, and wrote this
little poem of congratulations, kowtowing in homage to him, and wishing from afar
that Guanguan may live to an even riper old age. [YL]

17. Guanguan's wife. [BH]

a breaking wave's rank promotes you to squad leader
leading wanton tenderness   multiplying zero in a poem
refresh refresh   what's 90-year-old   what's 900-year-old
a lifetime's mess   nothing but a tiny little flight into exile
to a rhyme washed clean last night   sing your Airs of the States[19]
play your Pacific Ocean zither   mess mess   called big
little lamp lighting the starry sky   messy-mess   called beautiful
Master says   these tattered clothes of mine   perfect fit for a refreshing
    world
call up Su Dongpo[20]   drunken sleep for a while   Heiya Heiya
drag him drag him   dragging every messy him   we're away home

---

19. A section of the ancient *Shi Jing* or *Poetry Classic* edited by Confucius himself, it was believed in Imperial times. [BH]

20. Translator's note: Famous poet, painter, calligrapher, and gastronome Su Shi (1037–1101). [BH]

海上家书

Letter Home from at Sea

Dedicated to my mother and father
    'death is our new home now'
        (from *Mother*)[21]

the candle flame doesn't heed the clumsy hand
it recoils   like the day   hides in the cyclamens
and hides in the laughter in your eyes a photograph retains
flickering as ever   this moment is a tiny little Heaven Pond
superimposed waves folded into ice's form
        only death is our new home
        poetry is kindling the Eternal Flame   I am kindling the Eternal Flame

after a forty-four-year separation still burning in the same winter night
two faces   leaning to one side and both engraved by light
without looking back I know they're writing a letter   outside the window
joined-up black surges into one joined-up sea
life is just one thin page   written all over with words   too small for the words
        only death is our new home
        a sick seabed   time and time again cleared

this moment   I am plural   we are singular
for the first time catching on the air the smell of departed souls mingling
first co-written letter home   posted from
a non-existent home   two names reaching memory
swollen into my name   side by side waves slap the little sea
        only death is our new home
        this mortal world is so small   a cold and lovely cinerary urn

---

21. See Yang Lian, tr. Brian Holton (1994) *Non-Person Singular,* p.77; also see Yang Lian, tr. Brian Holton (2002) *Notes of a Blissful Ghost*, p.46, and Yang Lian, tr. Brian Holton (2008) *Riding Pisces*, p.77. [BH]

containing all partings   consanguinity's candle leaves on the windowsill
a close-listening winter night   it has all come back
double darkness makes me visible   a child
delivered by pen-point   stamped with a blood group unalterable
a poem of reincarnation has a fragile pink dust-jacket   as temperature is
    so beautiful
        only death is our new home
        agonising as a dream   sweet as a dream

oh who   dying   sits in the hatched horizon
your deaths   cyclamens like a breeze scatter ash and bone
wither and fall into my arms   trip lightly into my arms
I   tongue of fleshly flame   where dear ones are golden and gone
lick up to sea and night   expose sea and night
        only death is our new home
        sounds of unrecognised weeping   drip blood as they wait for a name

18 January—5 February 2018

病毒隔离中的生日华尔兹（一——五）
Birthday Waltz in Virus Isolation (1——5)
(for YoYo)

1

home is a tower   each and every magnetic line of force
is circular   we're like two magnets breathing   close together
the faint spring breeze in the room revolves around the invisible centre of
    a circle
turn oh turn   creaking floorboards have greened into a skyline

departed souls are green too   departed souls register on birthdays
air heavy and sticky   think it's just pollen
leading lungs first out the left foot   to stride   to precisely trample
at reincarnation   who is embraced by dance music close enough to choke

as we skip round and round?   us or departed souls
squeeze into the notes   each asking   love
was soaked in what fluid never to let the darkness's elasticity go?

a trembling glass of water on a marble table
handed through the void   the ash-grey crust is breath
pellucid   is a whole lifetime precipitated into a day for you

2

the purple lily magnolia opens five fingers to grab blue sky
grab the dark in the tower   dance   every round
downwards   the virus composer assigns the orbit of perfume
the cinerary urn's music spills out of this day

and us   embraced and diving across so many Aprils
a beautiful dance partner   another birthday made into a buoy
faces death and ripples   every weightless lamp sweeping by like a galaxy
how many towers are collapsing in this tower

60

a tender perfume thorn pricks into a poem's rhythm
the poem pricks into flesh   fibrous roots that coughed up blood take us
jumping into the whirlpools of departed souls before and behind

a handful of hurriedly mingled   ash   don't know whose
enchants my eyes   when catastrophes are beyond counting   just remember
it's you who lies in the crook of my arm

3

sheet music hides in the depth of the eye   and waits for distance to be
    erased
a hand on a waist pulls the curve of time
a smell you know best   distinguishes
this body   revolves into shapes overlapped

a new born face is pressed up against a face holding death in
the dance steps haven't changed   the departed souls have skipped into an
    avalanche
sunlight's bizarre carnival   inverted oxygen masks cover new green
we no longer need bad news from elsewhere

and the tomb of the street is attending a flowery class
leaves discover tongues licking a Good Friday oratorio
bad news has never been elsewhere

this tune has no ending
so many lives pumped out so many times
fungi in the throat   leaning on mouldy echoes

4

protective clothing of glass can't stop imagination
a tiny reality that broke out of the body-jail
neighbours bend over the window   faces shrunk to an invisible fence
over a night the empty blue sky air-drops so many fellow sufferers

a topic for philosophy   is death linking or disconnecting?
you and I wading on seabed sand   don't know
which shore we're on the verge of   the front of darkness bundling up bones
split open as they're cuddled into dazzling coral

every minute and second the road home looks more real
the circling road   endures a spiral stair in the tower
waves made by a couple   hammer into the universe's snow-white relative
        motion

I am your ventilator   and you are mine
a never-untangling drilled into a deep well of kisses
upward overlooks an imprisoned reflection

5

this birthday has seamlessly transitioned into an anniversary of departed souls
a room like a poem   a journey pivoting around its axis
spring scenery trampling its deathly pale calcified prototype
love   trampling deathbed's sharpness

the same day grows two tender green antennae
I am a bridge   its other end is on your body   aesthetics of
sacrifice   in another instant takes the bright beautiful flesh in its mouth
a white vastness of lung   left a waltz like dying words

tight linked   you   me   and departed souls
swarming into an endless dance   every time
as if inlaid in each other for the very last time

pellucid as a requiem   precipitating countless
lyrical and miserable prehistories   one hand melts in another hand's fuse
a beam of hard light passes through a locked-in stare

名字的诞生
Birth of a Name
(for Mo Huang)[23]

was the ocean at high tide outside Queshi[24] bleak enough?
that day   when we stood as a line of breakers
the agitating wind's howl in our collars   we saw without turning
the bay was leaving still with a hometown accent
to add to the skyline of Xiao Du and Yao Feng[25]   sunny words
are all the edge of the sky   white hair Old Gu painfully recited
recognising a seagull's foreign land   nearer than a hometown
and so unafraid   we drove over the big bridge   the army camp
the seawall stretched its finger   in dazzling nothingness
the lamplight for sale was embedded in black man-made night
every blown-up stone closer than a museum
that day   was the old town of Shantou so full of building sites bleak enough?
we strolled   in ghostly Live-In-Peace Alley house numbers woke
on YoYo's head   clematis of balcony rust blackening time's black
Shao Shan[26] looked up dumbfounded at banana leaves piercing the floor's
      green
carvings   curve how tender and lovely   still couldn't change
the shaky old house of life Please Keep Out
leaning on a bound and tied bamboo pole
roof endlessly crashing behind nailed-shut window bars   Suizi   Ming Di[27]
must also bow and admit their sins under the Crackdown on Crime slogan[28]
    (some night   dim streetlamps abruptly brought a ghost town to life)
where can ghosts migrate to?   the screen's memory

---

23. *Mo huang* means 'never desolate' but is a homophone of 'don't panic'. It's a nickname Yang and his friends gave to a friend's son. [BH]

24. Outside Shantou, Guangdong Province. *Que* is pronounced *chü-eh*. Queshi bridge, at 2,402 metres, is one of the longest cable-stayed bridges in the world. [BH]

25. 26. 27. The poet's friends. [BH]

28. Often translated as *Strike Hard*, these slogans and campaigns are a regular feature in China. [BH].

thinner than a photo   the sound of our trampling steps
has come back   is the dust with its armful of saltiness enough to reach
the final   nameless   a hot-pot was spitting steam
debating your existence   foster parents more seething than thrown into a
        poetry festival
that day   a table covered with offerings of the years
sacrificed   what gulped down wholly bleak   no longer afraid of bleak
a little person   a point of fall
a steaming-hot newly-invented weeping and wailing
sip a little *baijiu*[29] to keep company with red-eyed Old Gu
no panic   no rush

---

29. Strong (40-50%) spirit typically made from sorghum. [BH]

汕大，封存的家书
Shantou University: A Sealed Letter Home

you walk among the girls   along the starry sky
spill lines of magnetic flux   the end-of-lesson bell
releases sparks   a tree-shade trajectory
brings you closer   verifies the astronomy in my eyes

the pink silk tree's pretty colours on your nose-tip walk too
on the napes of so many necks   young girls' fragrance
swaying jade pendants   little sea of books in armpits
light sparkles on waves   youth is a kind of power   shyness too

you walk amongst the girls   shadows holding
the loveliest shadow   inside I'm all printed moonwalks
floating grows into a poem just shedding its placenta

bring with little lakes   bridge   the reflected ridge line
you are an imagination   sipping my visions
a tiny milky-smelling curriculum
leads me to the study immeasurable depths of seeing
is there really a space-time that can press down like rain-clouds
to split the weighty blood ties between stone and stone?
amongst the hustle and bustle of the girls
in a moment's longing shrunk to the starry sky
you walk by   you will never vanish from my vision

19 April 2019

绚丽的不可解封之诗
Magnificent Non-Deblockable Poem

1

the whole of life is a one-time approach
a pass in the hills   a pass of snow
a person   split apart   a soaking wet pass

the whole of life   is hearing a pink sawblade
dragged across a void   same winter same dance

the road goes north
who is conceiving and planning it?   a twilight stair rising step by step
evening hung on a wire ripples our far gaze
keeps grinding the tiny hills down
cold pooled in the throat   fragmentary as a kind of beauty

oh see   saw teeth on your body finely bite into life's desolation

whose artwork is displayed in the room
incessantly seeping darkness and the smell of blood   displayed in an artwork
our breath nestles side by side into our breath   swings back here again and
        again

entrance is exit   fated
to carve and polish the same crystallised teardrop

an empty chestnut tree is encrypting a horned moon crying out in pain
a corridor is leading a womb   a pouting egg
holds the world in its mouth   oh skip   the dance can't stop   the
        weeping can't stop
glazed tiles of flesh take shape little by little   only for swallows
existing one time   we fly in   silently shatter a while
sink into tepid non-blockable curses

until a love song's contours emerge from inner eternal night

2

the wild peach flower says nothing   just holds up a human face

springtime elegantly scrawls you
springtime elegantly imprisons you

dripping wet time is focused on a cheekbone
a stone that has endured for generations
leaves a smiling silhouette behind

charmingly pretty   like a spirit fox

leaning into the green behind us   just like a poem at this moment
opening line by line   hiding love at greater depths

a portrait is infinite in variety   a mass of lines
practised a thousand years   you are painted   written   read out
the silence I swallow drags nine tails[30]
and the apparition of a vital organ   comes   carrying invisible thought

exposed just so beneath the sky of the worst news
carefully counts the destinies of the worst news   soft saw teeth mouthing
     a little flesh
the funnel of the eye leaks a world   springtime storing up
desire   never let slip to polish every wound
a peach tree grown from a spasm of pain makes the hearts of the dead
     suddenly bloom
so near it's like unreal   like exactly my own secret

you use my thousand-year stare to walk away from me

leaving only a poem like a horizon spread underfoot
springtime is never used up   elegance is unchangeable

---

30. The nine-tailed spirit fox is a common figure in Chinese myth and folklore.
[BH]

听茶 (一)
Hear Tea (1)

a stretch of blue shuts its own worries tight   leans back
on a little gravel path   sea of clouds   Heaven's Lake poured full
a stretch of blue boils a splash of spring water in the eye
scenery shrouded in primal mist   chasing sea level in your body   drifts

      close your eyes   there is a string in the eardrum
      scalds you hurts you   an instant of perfume explodes becoming space

then this morning has been heard   blue
also has its footsteps climbing the hill   in the old house of a tree
a homely voice never can finish picking   high cold leads you to grow a tender
    shoot
camellias embedded in fading dreams hesitate to speak

      limpid reflections   who is not overlooked by water?
      a cup of the most exquisite tea left beside a poem

like a sunny musical instrument   reads drifting names aloud
drinking among a vast sea of faces is also drifting   an eyeful
leaf veins run with sap   oh every drop suck and taste a drop of you
pain of beauty   pain of return

      slowly swallow a whole sleepless night
      slowly swallow a sung   obliterated infinite distance

silently say   no need   taste as you hear
hear as you think   a waft of perfume melts into flesh and blood
has deleted flesh and blood   blue blue arrival at a mountaintop
in Heaven's Lake a rippling poem never leaves

      you endure echoes   a skyline all alone in the world
      up-curling focal length aims at salt on the wound

9 January 2020

听茶 (二)
Hear Tea (2)

hearing a dream is like hearing a colour
the moon always hangs low over two teacups in air
your Double Springs[31]   your music   daily
fallen   deeper darkness always sings with too much pathos

      let a little sea soak the innermost heart
      steep cliffs underfoot   a raging sea comes closer with every step

cast-iron balcony railings are also a sky-blue word
never spoken   everything wrapped up tight
dancing steps on last night's wilderness incomparably quiet   incomparably noisy
who's there   stepping on a green leaf to flutter gracefully away?

      is there someone in the perfume of tea   or no one?
      overflowing soft heart   delicately sniffs its own misfortune

a dream lets you endlessly sit down into
a bashful body   lets diffused growth rings
diffuse the spherical back-swinging storm   your black-necked crane
shrieks with its skeleton   who says elegance can't boil over?

      a naked non-existence   the instrument's sound
      entangles   your blood-dripping tenderness

still held in darkness's mouth   predestined
perform a blinded musical score   to hear tea is to hear you
where is the drifting abyss diving to?   how far the sound of a shattering fall?
the world has learned to mumble to itself like a mind

      darkness inexhaustible   only a kiss
      a cup has passed time and space to lightly rest on red lips

14 January 2020

---

31. *Double Springs Reflect the Moon:* a famous air for *erhu* (the Chinese 2-string fiddle) by blind fiddler Abing. [BH]

念湖

Lake Longing[32]

(A photography exercise)

a lake is the same shape as the worst possible news
bigger than life   bigger than death
you walk the lakeside   everyone walks the lakeside

the camera in your hand testing the black water
an era of mist   chestnuts go far like a crane
backward grow the cries of migration

waves deeper than you endlessly calibrate
a dream's focal length   morning wakes
empty clay walls staring at a temperature of zero

millimetre by millimetre pushing your shadow into a trance
your prettiness   sinks a little in holding your breath
and adds a little more too

thinking and wishing are like forgetting
what leaked away   absent   pure pure white
mist   where is its shore?

soaked only once in slowly exhausted heartbeats
do shadows offer ruin as collateral?   shadows are ruin
lake   gobbles down 1/1000 of a second

---

32. There is a pun in the title, *Nian Hu* 《念湖》 – *nian* 念 translates a complex
of ideas including *long for/miss, think of, read aloud, thought, idea*, etc, while *hu* 湖
is simply *lake*. However, there is also a Nian Lake or *Nian Hu* 念湖 in Yunnan
Province, which is a nature reserve for the Black-Necked Crane (*grus nigricollis*),
and is where many other species of migrant birds overwinter. It has been described
as 'paradise for a photographer'. [BH]

depth of field that chokes nothingness
collapses   stores up a long sigh
lies waste   nothing is left

an era absolutely dead sparkles with phony wavelight
multiplies the worst possible news   already is the one and only worst
    possible news
locks you down   collages you

overlooking water   with no you
a song of exile endlessly performed
press the shutter   a reflected world takes its revenge

19 January 2020

白千层

A Thousand White Layers[33]

a deep pain can only be wordless
with my skin's thousand waves   thousand snowdrifts
wordlessly strip a springtime open

spring colours of a last goodbye   ripped up layer by layer
a lump of flesh hides endlessly in anguish
rips invisible pain   thread–fine incessant

see thrashing   see snuggling
a tattered story   not too much and not too little is lovesick longing
snuggle into growth rings   carefully count your own breaking

a thousand white layers   new green like ruin and desolation
one leaf silently chases someone's back view
ruin and desolation pulled in the hands   that skyline

rumpled lawn   rumpled lakelight
read into me   read out a thousand of you
lakelight glittering   holds the same internal injuries together

a morning the same spot hasn't moved
when tender caresses are deepest   watching her go is the only lesson left behind
brightness of morning's death   one kiss

emptied body of thawed snow
waking tears   held in eye sockets not there
a body stands quiet at the roadside   children all learning ruin

27 April 2019

---

33. The Chinese name for *Melaleuca alternifolia*, the tea tree, is literally a thousand white layers. [BH]

御花园·零与夜
Imperial Garden. Zero and Night

the silence of the tomb   tightly gripped in a beauty's hands
Our Imperial Self [34]   empty courtyards   pools all reflections

been massaged been frigged   dome snow-white
a new moon on a body of ochre marble erect

played enough   sticking lazily to nothingness

zero is born so   like a dream of numbers
dreaming a pool downward building another palm tree

dreaming you walking out from a reflection   night behind you
records a single unbearable *AAH*

with   what flicked across the water   Our eyes unable to look away

---

34. 朕 *zhèn* the Royal We, a 1st person pronoun used only by an Emperor. [BH]

御花园·孔雀
Imperial Garden. Peacock

that bird appears at a high palace window
an emerald star   stepping on mortal din
a living crevice   tears open the ancient doctrines of dust

under a tiny crown
children keep on baring black legs
mothers still flashing jewel eyes
hurt that deserves hurt   collapse that deserves collapse

who should be exquisite and flamboyant   so blooming
for Our Imperial Self   a flower-like a female sightline
inlaid in the sky   like a poem not joined to your lives and deaths

crushed the world with a glimpse of nothingness

御花园·牡蛎
Imperial Garden. Oyster

Our Imperial Self only wants that living thing   a crack
slightly opened   glimpses a slippery wet ocean

pools in the mouth   a ball of fruit pulp jerking and growing
slightly salty   fresh as flowers' fragrance
sea viscera steep yellow–white   pucker
also as if prised open   the harem hides in Our body

you moan   trickle and drip   peel Us a glittering thorn

to dip in a lemon all night long
live in a downward-creeping duct   We have fallen for
a keenly-relished fate that tightly grips from inside

御花园·铜舟
Imperial Garden. Bronze Boat

the sail we have cast   slices the wind with warm veins open

swelling forward   a poem defines a bloom of spindrift
the prow gently rises   pushes into
the relations between all phenomena   a bronze seagull squawks from the
        masthead
bronze salt   streaks a full moon with rust

the world swept clean of dust by imagination
a tiny masthead light finds a symbol

hidden in sailors' tiny   deaf-mute shadows
a deck that never refuses yet more delusion
pulling you   voyages on a hand's lines of latitude and longitude

御花园·墨乐
Imperial Garden. Music of Ink

one drop of ink passes sentence of life or death   one drop
cloud and mist suddenly rising   Our Imperial Self sits in the Garden of
    Reincarnation

Our stamen   laps the bitterness of ashes
one museum displays Our charred lands and waters
one word   holds the joy and sorrow of breath

We spray   a flurrying white paper of girls blooms and withers

ink's spirit can't see   can only make you hear
ink's spirit all through the theatre   weasel-hair brushes dip into destiny
flutter and dance   built-up black flying white as snow
each pubic hair We strum gives off a rare perfume

until the final roar   promises endless silence

御花园·来德之风
Imperial Garden. Laide's Wind[35]

harshly file this wrinkled wilderness smooth   bushes   roads
cypress trees' green all slant in the same direction
Our Imperial Self's brushstrokes push you into the raging wind and waves

whirl around tightly hook uphill and down   spasming in your flesh
flee your skin   generate
that sunset and cold every instant on Mother Earth

there are no words unable to be overlooking
hugging the window deathly tight
We   rub a blank into rare blossom again

just one magic breath needed   a world will withdraw back to most
    beautiful nakedness

---

35. Zeng Laide (*b*. 1956), Sichuan Province, famous painter and calligrapher. [BH]

御花园·玉圭

Imperial Garden. Jade Tablet[36]

axle of stone   a sort of bottle-green Our Imperial Self adores
propping you up from inside as you spin
a pure form   the wilder the storm the stiller the inner heart

tongue tip sticking a tiny bit up and out
carries spat-out words   soaks swallowed words
on branch tips a whole world's leaves hang and rustling shiver

a thousand moonlit nights pinched between Our fingers
a thousand you breathe at a subtracted margin
hold together a gushing   condensed   life and death

beyond an extreme elegance   we simply have nothing

---

36. An elongated tablet with a pointed end, used like a sceptre by ancient rulers.
[BH]

御花园·石器时代
Imperial Garden. Stone Age

the time that stones sigh out bit by bit finds
that body shape   lying on tussocks of grass
Our Imperial Self chops off your sex

unbearable moonlight like hands   back and forth drags
a black rope wearing a round hole in soft jade

the deep past lists   densely-packed knife-blades and lips
but there was only one piece   made your flowering seasons always thrive
held Us tight and didn't let go   We forbid you to let go
stones collapse endlessly from that side they piled up into mountains themselves

rely only on that lump that lacked flesh on the other side
balancing until now

御花园·最后的
Imperial Garden. Final

door shut   garden calm and still
stamens   oozing in a fragrant flooded drowning cell

lock up Our Imperial Self   the walls are you   outside the walls is you too
a word is limitlessly enormous   the world is smaller than an instant

green of leaf-veins crystalline as a jade carving
the final mating can't be seen   can't be stopped
the final moan moulded into a scalding instrument of torture

We order the far mountains   cloud and snow to relocate into skin
one night of glamour gouges out all other seasons
use up humiliation   the having been loved glamour of night after night

when silence is reached   a lifetime's distress-calls bloom inside

罪恶研究

Researching Evil

PREFATORY NOTE: The foundations of this poem lie in two important events in 2022: first, the Ukraine War; second, China's Chained Woman. She was a sex slave kidnapped and sold by traffickers to Shifeng County, Xuzhou, Jiangsu Province. When she was found her tongue had been cut out, all her teeth extracted, and around her neck was an iron chain: her psychological state and her powers of speech had been grossly impaired and she had been left with severe disabilities; she had also been raped and had borne eight children as a result of 'traditional' treatment by the peasants who bought the use of her. This incident has reduced 'Mother' to the dirtiest word in the vocabulary of the Chinese language. After this was exposed on the internet, it set off a tidal wave of popular anger, gaining tens of millions of hits, shares and comments in no time at all, as well as fierce attacks on the official media and the legal system which cover up underworld vice. Since the 1989 Tiananmen Massacre in Beijing, this is the first time the Chinese people have exploded in a massive movement of spiritual enlightenment. I have called it 'An off-street Tiananmen'.

white snow can be an infernal machine too
to crush   so many dying of a life
so many ghosts released by one death
Pushkin's tears
Tsvetaeva's tears
pile on the shoulders of bronze statues   unmelting metal
pawning rhymes of nothingness   dragged through
the hearts set up as empty shells
a poem might also be   (can only be)   the mass grave of poetry
burial locking up pain too deep for tears
the same early spring ten thousand miles away
nailed into a collarbone   a catastrophe
drowns another catastrophe   recycled flesh and blood

recycled into forgetting   so many ghosts
still crawling from resurrection-emptied graves
motionless ruins reduced to rubble in their mouths
making us mistakenly think
an era of despair is new

why has this muddy and inert road no ending?
this grey-green conifer forest   gaze ice-cold
why has it only left rancid meaning the same as the pale sun?
charming Katya   Natasha   shrapnel sticking to their chests
like new-picked blood mushrooms
is this the homecoming you were all waiting for?
a bird flushed into flight from someone else's hometown
was it granted the power to appear in your dreams?
big-eyed skulls gaze straight at bombed-out streets
only one question   why destroy all this?
how much longer must this downhill ladder go   till it arrives at
the terror of children   a vacuum like a fireball exploding
hanging deep in the heart   could the world have been blinded by fire
        long ago?

that tunnel in a mother's body
leads to chains   leads to lying
a vast grand piano smashed to pieces every day
ocean waves slap   human needlegrass shivers in the wind
mother   the humblest word   the filthiest word
leads to layers of bloodstain strata
and another dumbstruck morning
watching her locked on a butchered mother-tongue
watching us locked in the bomb shelter of shame
the same tattered shirts and crawling on the ground   scrape away human
        bubbles
the umbilical tunnel lets us witness a road under guard
dug into our bodies   corpses folded onto corpses
forever empty   oh listen   the wind's wail has no history
a species that can't save mothers doesn't even deserve doomsday

but this really is doomsday
a maggot wears countless shades of grey   shrivelled names
on every stone squat hordes of refugee ghosts
this is spring   the worst bloodstained news sprouts faster than green leaves
bloodstains cover over bloodstains   our dried-up surfaces
almost equal to fictions   a loss before our very eyes
the phantoms of home scatter and vanish faster than tear-filled eyes
a mother's used-up vagina   must still go on being used up
draw a planet's orbit the non-distance between death and death
a never-past March asks   is there truly a way back?
Spring's face that leaves behind some enchantment   being clearly and
        clearly stroked
like a false emblem

a crime   can't remember the beginning but only the weight of shadows
fills in none of Death Row but only human-shaped shell holes
stops at the shape of a sleeper left by a deserted road
the dirty hand on the red button lightly twists the stamen of destruction
twirls the topic on the dinner table   glasses and plates daintily jingle
corpselike tongues licking child-charring fires
timidity so tasty   saves your body
makes it quietly and softly putrify   saves your silence
explosively chokes your lungs   saves a life seeping away each second
it isn't anything at all   but crime itself
staring at the madness of a branch of peach blossom   like madness
created by fingers   March collapsing   March soaked in sweat
seeing us tied to a ghost's bed   falling further than ghosts into
nowhere   no word more shameless than innocence
no little hand stretching from the soil that hasn't gripped my body-odour
no iron umbilical cord that hasn't pulled out a bone-grey river
it knows no other future   but disappearance itself
disappearing in the shocking sight of a branch of peach blossom
beauty layer on layer   palms all sticky with farewell train windows
a whistle blows everything away

this is an unwriteable poem   an impossible poem
there is no one in this poem   all that's left is everyone

facing the mirror of crime   the mirror of evil
Li Shangyin's tears fall independently of ours
who is who's counterfeit   the illusion cursing in the mirror
recognise the only division is real   shattered on a reef
mended in thick fog   feeble echoes
wiped and wiped away again   from white snow to peach blossom   hear
poetry reciting with no heart   a history arises from an empty shell
painlessly walks out of itself

we have always lived like this

反安魂曲
Anti-requiem[37]

(for my younger brother Yang Yue, who passed away on 14 December 2022)

the World of the Dead is infinite   but which departed soul can be at rest?
no instrument can tell this cold[38]   day of a house emptied
brother   you sink into an interminable crowd
another car screams by at speed   that sprint
hits a dead end   an ICU
lays bare innumerable finish lines   eyes staring and still
brother   where are the smallest dying words frustrated?

a final clot of sucked-out   phlegm hard and dry
sucks up how many lives?   a white sheet
like a seabed   sketches a body's craggy outline
that emaciation   hurts 1960 howling in agony
that dumb silence   leaks 2022 incomplete
both ends of your slender rope are broken
a drop of water   not a sea   futilely hugging sea's bitter salinity

brother   no pain in death   a catastrophe gave you pain
a huge area suddenly erased   a huge area emptied
an all-pervading medicinal taste years and months can't treat
all your poisoned fates   nicknamed untimely death
a blinded lingering winter   by whose hand led
whipped by whom   fallen into an impossible rebirth
the Devil and Yama[39] both put on human shape

to lock down empty streets in the whole city
lock down the way out of life   the way out of death   a blood drop
didn't flow   from hell to hell already   black is white only
in Mother's eyes the shame of words falls as snow
nights of Siberia   Wuhan   Jiabiangou[40]
white has long been black   brother   an underlying disease called our era
on the Bridge of No Return ruin locked infinitely nearer[41]

zero meaning   gobbles down each zero fate
zero   twists all the unwilling   freezes a heart
your horizon is an electrocardiogram flatlined
a zero moment   pulverises day and night   pulverises ancient and modern
the First Seventh Day has passed   one by one like lock gates more sevens
are waiting for you   a bone-chilling nothingness in a backward glance
echoless history bangs down its iron signet

brother   the cursed first light keeps your desolation company
your firewood   firewood for all of you   up to the heavens heaped
I see the ashes of the departed souls   ashes escaped
full of rancour   inescapable misery
a cinerary urn always waking   nowhere ensconced
a requiem can only sing crushed fragments that can't be soothed away
a last farewell   absolutely like hopelessness severed

the day's toxic petals dry and cracked   flayed bare
a cold hard iron bed pillages a world
your death lays bare a horizon dying and dying once more
the mother tongue of pain   housing the homeless ghost
din of forgetting ear-piercingly scrapes at the future
brother   no way for this waste pile to be at rest   shouldn't be at rest
behind the tight-shut iron door empty and black are the borderless angry billows

24 December 2022
The day my brother was cremated.

---

37. The form is quite musical: each stanza is rhymed AABAABA, 7 stanzas of
7 lines, based on the Chinese Seven Sevens tradition of remembering the dead. [YL]

38. See W.H. Auden, 'In Memory of W.B. Yeats': 'What instruments we have
agree/The day of his death was a dark cold day.' [YL]

39. Yama, Lord of the Underworld, and Judge of the Dead. [BH]

40. Labour camp in the Badain Jaran Desert of NW Gansu province during
the Anti-Rightist Campaign of 1957-61, where some 3000 prisoners were sent for
'Reform Through Labour' (*laogai*). Around 2500 died from starvation, with neither
food nor agricultural supplies provided. This is still a taboo topic in China. [BH]

41. The bridge every departed soul has to cross to be reincarnated. [BH]

二，组诗

SEQUENCES

轮回·灵骨塔 (98行)
Reincarnation – Stupa (98 lines)
(for my father, as the world is isolated by a virus)

1

the twelfth-floor window is bright and silent
taking his pulse   counting his breaths
a shaft of light is scattering in slanting afternoon shadow
the buildings are a Forest of Steles   each half lost to the dark
his name floats in fluid tainted with golden dust
slipping down drop by drop   shattering unheard into this instant
the messy waves on a bed coated in body odour
batter into me   two worlds juxtaposed on each side of the window
a century in name only like a wave of the hand   eyes barely open
ten thousand miles away a cell phone records water stains drying on the ebb
    tide

2

can't imagine my hand not holding his   to feel
his temperature withdraw little by little   hiding in a wound
an isolated spring is still an unpostponable spring
guttural sounds trundle behind his mumbling lips   with outside the window
green spreading to the Tianjin TV Tower equally abstract   fragile last words
prop up a man waiting for a miracle that isn't going to appear
his books neatly lined up   his music collectively silent
where can footsteps on Middle Lakeside Road still be walking to?
I can't imagine my hand hasn't touched time to slowly restore
its essential nullity   as a stupa locks a whole-body window up tight

3

a second is so small   fingertips just pinch a weakening heartbeat
a second is so big   a whole history tempered into its acuity
that steep slope we hadn't noticed   with a sort of pallor
rising higher   climbed the cliff of a drop of bloody urine
a gasp of administered oxygen chokes solid water

water chokes sea   when has the difficulty of struggle ever fallen apart?
his head pillowed on an unseen knife-edge   revealed once to slash
every second only validates the pain of the real-name system once
delineates my horizon line   sunset flashes on a window far away
the afterglow that embraces me has neither limit nor end

4

all darkness summed-up into a night in his room
on that bed   the taste of affection wraps me like year after year
daffodils in a dream   that shadow bent into a warm hollow
neither big nor small it fills me   the stillness of this moment
brewing ears in a storm ten thousand miles away   this no sleeping
exchanged for a piece of old jade's waking to chant a millennium oozing blood
scuffling as it chases him   the pacing in the room can be incessant too
a whiff of perfume   brings jade-green to fume a bitter cold outside the
     window
makes me settle a lifetime's emptiness into this hallucination
I can never return to   the longer the better   to avoid the coughing of
     coming day

5

the window handcuffs abstract   Eternal Lamps
the window   reminds the dark of official seals   the dark of the same being
Keep Out is the only reality   the starry sky passes him
passes me again   the same day switched on and off
yet unchangeable   light-years' neglect
like a hole in a corner covered with patched pink plastic sheeting
has another kind of elegance   he sits up only to see the twilight
and non-existent me   another tiny wave on the stairs
tranquil love and tranquil relinquishing equally elegant
the 12th-floor stupa is solitarily flowering

6

a person is a stupa
a person seeks his own slowness through a ninety-eight-year-old quick march
the last hike displayed on the windowsill   always just about to
set out   sees a second hang sparkling on the bottle's lip

trembling   dripping   ninety-eight spring times a micro-tsunami
anniversaries stored in his body all graduated by seconds
the stopwatch nipping him   like the dark winding stair takes him in its
    mouth
every steady step   no destruction other than his own flesh and blood
descending onward   a spattering red sky between infinite pages
a person overtakes without motion the obediently returning world

7

virus and history both push me   far from
my arrival   seeing him on the cell phone screen
and seeing the poisonous air   the whistle of death
calling out to Du Fu[42]   lungs that can't squeeze onto the ward go vast
    and white on the road
and ashes pile up   pinch and shape yellow-white viscera
no need to say goodbye   endlessly say goodbye
through a tightly-sealed window   tongues of flame   lap
an ending of assumptions   on TV gaudy retrospective channels
change direction at any moment   fester into news of the pandemic again
the worst news won't be past   won't sympathise with me being a living
    ghost

8

Black Ox City Road   Middle Lakeside Road   Expressway   Friendship
    Mall
one after the other drift up rugged seabeds   neon advertising
fish-eyes recharging batteries   staring at who the puddle of night is
faint rippling   his window overlaps my window
which one isn't a lens   poised to shoot
after death isolated by a moment   this infinitely near spring time green
also infinitely far   embedded in a century   obliterating a century
this old dog's weary eyes lazily suck phosphorescence in
not worth rising for a favourite fake   we grip tight
to the crazy gale that only ever left everything stripped and blank

---

42. Du Fu (712-770 CE), China's greatest poet. [BH]

9

a double nothingness of past and future sandwiches the glass
his gaze and mine collide   break off   a transparent
non-existence   the endless fall from the twelfth floor
a teardrop in the corner of the eye is something I've never seen before
one hand   apparition of through   a gentle pat
the deepest dream   changed into a difficult kiss blown once in a lifetime
protesting against all distance   yields to the final distance
every organ falling back to open a landscape of zero data
sharing both sides gazing in vain into the distance
each one silently shattering their own shards

10

each one cries for help from their own stupa   ten thousand miles away
water stains on the beach   write go back home   write hope
unfinished spring leaks slowly down   a scene of green ruin
thickens a far journey inch by inch between pitch black tree trunks
melody isn't the glare of words   it sings pain directly
every line equivalent to impossible   in love with the impossible
leaving a Stone Age message   it rives open disappearance in a cellphone
the twelfth-floor window is bright and silent

倒退的历史诗——给香港

Poems on Turning Back History

for Hong Kong

1

ocean waves polished snow-bright   matching helmets   shields
gulf like a laid-down high-rise   collapses into
the dark rising and falling   a neon other shore
lightly rippling   the mirage embraces us and our rippling
one incarnadine-feathered seagull bobs by
one million glass curtain walls polished snow-bright   reflect history

2

once again   we fall into a death-trap
for a perfectly ordinary morning   we put on
the bloody clothes of thirty years ago   running bodies
turn into sea breezes   the black of gas blocks all directions
a street has no beginning   only countless masked endings are left
trip and fall   who hasn't experienced a shattered life in the word *fate*?

3

everybody is a barricade   a road block
fiercely blocking ourselves   suffering wounds not worth it
enduring unendurable pain   fear   filled-up fire hoses
spit bitter salty blue   inescapable rain
always a swollen square   like a damp seedbed
death's desire madly sprouts carrion

4

once again   the convex lens of the ocean's ancient teardrop
weeps our tears   those resigned to their fate   recognise
storm's onomatopoeia   retelling the pitter-patter of ruin
hearts   wake at morning to die and die again pushing at walls
dark that motionless struggles   carefully sculpted to its limits
flight and pursuit are the same gesture

5

you all have a history class
        we have time that has been excised
you all display a constellation of skulls
        we gouge eyes out and join shadows
all your bronze goblets dazzle bodies
        our blood has been brewed into aesthetics

6

does the eyeball's bubble only see something when it bursts?
where does a port filled with the stink of dead fish sail to?
isn't senility shrivelled back into the past preposterous?
who is the submarine Mandelstam surfacing to meet?
how do steel vines intercept curses honed in the heart?
a bad poem   does it include a worse reality?

7

the glass canyon overflows with multicoloured water
turbulent yet silent   shoving at the shore
glass sky like an endlessly fallen landmass
multicolour pouring rain   collapses the feel of snow in the south
glass snow-bright   every reflected junction reversing into
the grave's dead corner   opens out in multicoloured mushrooms

8

a foundling of time
unsure if it's water or glass
coldly shoots light   delivers blank solids
in the hillside graveyard my headstone is damp
my name is damp   alive and climbing to
indifferent desolate absolute heights

9

the ocean's wilderness on all sides
strangles a tiny islet of people   throats black and blue
the old wound   silting up a midnight that acts calm

terror needs this corner   darkness
the thicker the better   saltwater-soaked it skips questions
what times?   whose shame?

10

imagine one face beside a sea of faces   like a little shore
prettily rising   the daughter leads by the hand
a lost history bewildering to eye-witnesses
so many truncheons are driving time's cattle in circles
crowds with lost faces are fighting   tamping down the same dirty stains
in contrast to you   a torn scrap of paper flutters by quite alone

11

where can we still turn back to?
the tar underfoot splits   seawater surges pitch-black
pours back into us like we are poured back into
the neon waterfall ghosts abruptly switch on
the terracotta warrior insists on kneeling   looks forward two millennia
the bow and arrow he held vanished into thin air

12

glass gravestone gleaming among ocean waves   ruin escorts it
one more dying day gone missing   beforehand forgets it
the foamy self seeps into foamy others   painlessly erases it
poetry   a rusty ferry boat   to its heart's content invents it
rotted-out corpses goosestep   never lacking an anniversary to cheer it
ocean's one-page will and testament rolls alongside   never anyone reading it

韩退之中元节，或从四面八方坍塌到我们头上的时光
Han (Retreater) Yu's Hungry Ghost Day
Or, Time That Collapses onto Our Heads from All Sides

1

Chaozhou[43] is here   retreater retreater   where can you still
retreat?   beside your feet   ocean's snowdrift
this Blue Pass[44] is uncrossable   your decrepit
sacrificial crocodile falls into a crocodile's mouth
your 8,000-league road like a tape measure   with the diameter of a heart
pack in Xi'an   Qinling Mountains[45]   the sob of a dying 12-year-old
     daughter
retreater retreat   you mostly retreat but can't go beyond one step's gnash
     of teeth
cold rain under the eaves of every courier station   condenses into ocean's
single bitter salty drop   Chaozhou is here   tides ebb and flow
between night and morning   third moon trudging   eighth month wasted
a life's epitaph written and rewritten again
a handful of dry bones on a miasmal riverside   you only know when you
     reach the ocean
death's beauty is endlessly distant   where can the vastness
of the heart retreat to?   a mountain pass on the horizon
rising vertically   a dead-end seamless as fate's end
retreat to this place   Chaozhou is the terminus   life
cramped as the cliff seagulls must leap from
leaping into 819 CE's[46]   one question of where home is
scales of waves   wearing the hungry green of loath-to-leave crocodiles

---

43. In Guangdong Province, in the far south of China. Han Yu was exiled here 819-820 CE. [BH]

44. Near Xi'an, Shaanxi Province. [BH]

45. South of Xi'an, Shaanxi Province, the border between North and South China. [BH]

46. In 819 CE Han Yu was sentenced to death, after he wrote an anti-Buddhist (and pro-Confucian) polemic: the sentence was commuted to demotion and exile to Chaozhou. [BH]

wait for your imminent snow   astral prophecy   layers by the thousand
catches up with a thousand-layer tree[47]   silently swaying in ruin incalculable
growing down into a bottomless pit

2

the stone steps of demotion and exile   down and down again
wave-splattered   slope cold and icy
ghosts swallow and spit to welcome the poet in
to this poem   tonight is Hungry Ghost Day

buried in spindrift time swallowing and spitting
blue as faraway combusting phosphorescence
man-shaped paper ash light and dark flickering
poetry   absorbing fully-rounded blood and flesh

you and us   to be worn down to our limits
is to once experience a secret maturing
bougainvillea under the arches like a blackly beautiful word
slate-paved streets damply lift the sacrificial offering

both ends are the past   lines of verse confirming
ghosts waking   eyes of the worst news
void staring at void   from the little hilltop
look out over the dream in a dream of storms swirling

weaving the basket of the world   with mind's deftness
smoothing out this and that with death's dimness
twelve hundred years   an indulgence never repeated
one side green mossy   assassinated   rhymed

nowhere to retreat to   this corpse-stench beauty
lists the reincarnations on the great river in spate
an utterly black grammar   wipes tears wiped away
the flame tree has tightly locked up context

---

47. In Chinese the tea tree *Melaleuca alternifolia* is called thousand-layer tree.
[BH]

a roaring   unreal bearing
cave-in polishing cave-in   sea waves
smash sea waves   time leaking
engraves starlight that embraces skulls

Hungry Ghost Day   ghosts hold ghosts tight
look down on   looked-down on   only one ancient and modern
enduring the light in the eye written down   long since written
the vertiginous known takes us down to decline

3

so the ocean is just like love   throws a vast shadow
regardless of before and after   head and tail   you and me
only leaves you and me

a vermicular motion dressed in hides
a peculiar installation   like days filled with only one drop

in Chaozhou   *The Works of Han Changli*[48] is a slate with polished and
     shining corners
you've walked the streets of gates[49]   I've walked the streets of gates
ghosts have walked past the ash of Kaiyuan Temple[50] hoarded for a thousand
     years
grab a handful of ends finely ground with zeroes
a coral clock endlessly rewinds now
stone stuck in a dead end   when it caves in
collapsed under its own dead weight   an empty shell
carves out the flesh colour of a fake High Tang

the iron hooks that stick out all around have caught us
death all around   has hooked classical connotation
created an art perfect as viscera

---

48. Han Changli is another name by which Han Yu is known. [BH]
49. Paifang are memorial gates, similar to Japanese torii. [BH]
50. Kaiyuan Temple in Chaozhou, founded in 738 CE. Presumably the ash is from
incense burners. [BH]

in Chaozhou   the twelvemonth smell of roast chestnuts on street corners
twelvemonth seafood tables covered in spat-out skeletons
your deep moan is chewing as well   dive underwater   in blood
the sounds of collapse blacken and thicken in the bottom of teacups
retreat   I am your ghost   and you have long been mine
a rejection that can go neither forward nor back
nothing to do with logic   everything to do with the imagination of a
        skeleton snow-white
banished to poetry's dead angle
everyone's word   a precisely embedded doom
fallen into a tiny   bright horizon

time all around   nowhere to retreat
forced into the one and only horizon in our hearts

in Chaozhou   accept the love of an animal that died and was reborn
swell up   surge   breathe the shadows in animal breath all around
degenerate syllogisms   shattered syllogisms
slapped into this moment   history's doom has no touchable shape
life's doom leaves behind only a lamenting sigh
language's doom is to spasm once
panting under the skin   a typhoon is like a fake arabesque too
painful piercing of what's unspoken   one turbulence drowns you and me
spawning a verse's lust   periscoping from the seabed
1000 years passed   1000 years yet to come   a vermicular longing
a glass of bitter wine that can't be drunk dry

rough billows   sprout bloody ox bones   mooing sacrifices
all coming back

20 June 2019

高福里中元节，上海背影之歌
Hungry Ghost Day at South Gate
Or, A Song of the Back View of Shanghai

1

Changle Road pitch dark and silent as dead butterfly's wings
sycamore trees open their fingers   mercury streetlights imitate the mist
old dream pipes are leaky

I walk   beer bottle for navigator   the blazing heat on Ruijin Road
lost in the blazing heat of the whole world

roadside   woman's voice in the shadows
'Whae ir ee eftir?' [51]

2

midnight's hour hand blocks in the double vastness before and after
my shoulder blocks in two days of blackness
coming out of Imperial Gardens   neon has taken its make-up off   faces
colour changed   hang on the invisible nail of the river breeze
my blown-around alien land wanders up to this door
South Gate   unfamiliar iron railings open for a son as usual

3

number 51 or number 52? a window drops out
from a hidden world   the lane leads me to this point
stops beyond the wall   watching your back view from a distance
across the neighbours' deathly silence like across a cast-iron window frame
                              my darkness keeps on forging

---

51. In this poem, Yang Lian inserts phrases in the dialect of Shanghai, which is as far from the Modern Standard Chinese of Beijing as Spanish is from Italian. I have taken the liberty of using my native Border Scots where he has used Shanghai Hua. The English sense is *'Who are you looking for?'* [BH]

a seductive sketch   a young girl carries
a little womb   still bicycles off into the far distance
the other side of the window in forever snuffed-out lamplight
South Gate turns round   Greater Shanghai turns round   (uncle says)
the Unicorn Kid[52] lived in Row 1   a hoarse cloud dangling from his voice
the Great World on Row 4[53]   the manager was called Ding   his finger
    pushed buttons
watching in a daze the Row 3 back door   Li Dashen   my maternal
    grandfather
your father   back view leading back view   disappeared into the room
dream factory   *'Div ee ken the time?'*[54]   a scrapped horizon

the window's postcard is filled with time's written code
I see you standing by the window   I can't see you standing by the window
I'm looking the other way   a bunch of old bundled electric wires
still humming in pursuit of the rippling patterned skirt of youth
mither   you don't see me   the window leans enchantingly on nothingness

4

Shanghai Museum   an underground garden of lamplight

jade *cong* tubes bottle Xin Tiandi[55]   shake bleeding that is thousands of
    years late

stuffed eyeballs scattered all around

---

52. *Qilin Tong* was the stage name of the actor Zhou Xinfang (1894-1975), one of the great masters of Peking Opera. He was imprisoned during the Cultural Revolution, and died while still under house arrest. [BH]

53. i.e. *Da Shijie*, the famous Shanghai arts and entertainment centre. [BH]

54. Shanghai dialect, 'What time is it?' [BH]

55. 琮 *cong* (pron. *tsoong*) are prehistoric artefacts of unknown function, tubes with a square outer section and a circular inner section. They appear from the Neolithic onward, mostly in jade or pottery. Xin Tiandi ('New World') is the renovated 19th-century residential area around Madang Road, the most expensive in China. [BH]

sunset and underpants   rocking a body empty in the wind

little brushes reveal a newly-excavated cinema

day   is only the name night's mumbling desires

5

South Gate   the archaeological site of my self
the local accent is yours   the darkness is mine
mither open yir mou an speak   turn into someone else
hou wad ee say't   hou'll ee can finn this airt?[56]
appearing in a dream   is the opposite direction too   from one person
turn back a ghost halfway   late afternoon dim as if fictionally back-lit
tight up against a little rust-streaked locked-up iron door
the sound of a piano has a back view too   embedded in cracks on the wall
a smear of moss silently grown into the grace of writing by a fountain pen
in a son's photo album   every page is a play within a play
turned over   the yellow-faced Hutuo River[57] plays castanets day and
     night
on the embankment you are arm in arm with a son   with a bag   a smile
hadn't you lost the style SJU[58] couldn't remake?
the son's poetry you also gave birth to   South Gate
turns to bury itself in a north wind that couldn't care less about right and
     wrong
a 'home' retrieved   every brick and tile like fifty-year-old rickets
but heartbeats   breath can't retrieve   concrete floor of dawn
throw out the endless opening in a pair of gold-rimmed glasses
January 7th 1976   the heart of winter
blocked at absolute zero

---

56. Shanghai dialect, 'Mother, open your mouth and speak'; 'How to say it...
how will you be able to find this place?' [BH]

57. The Hutuo rises in Shanxi Province and flows into the Bohai Gulf near
Tianjin. [BH]

58. St John's University was an Anglican university in Shanghai, 1879-1952. [BH]

the air is a revolving door   Mr Zhang comes over
a blue suit flaps across the alley   red trainers step on flames
stop outside number 52: *'Ir ee eftir Li Dashu?*
A kent him the best in this close, Li Dashu sellt this hous
ti ma faither' [59]

        the spark of surprise pulls in a back view
seventy years   like yesterday in his mouth
a non-existent little boy   couldn't have taken *mither*'s hand
but from legend comes   the four-eyed Maker of Letters [60]
talks the world into a story of shadows   shadow strings
knot a net of shadows: *'Here on the second floor   there's a big living room*
dining room   bedrooms   kids live in the attic   (mither in bed!)
the maid in the garret   right   your grandfather's furniture
stored for many years with our family'
        words wipe away time   leave behind poetry
make a life of shadowses [61] again: *'The two big carved doors here were taken away*
at the time of the big steelmaking [62]   *after that we just used the back door'*
Li Dashen also died in a little room pitch-dark and depressing as the back
      lobby
tenement courtyards of Beijing   full of cinders and slogans
the Maker of Letters   made Shi Dongshan's Shi   Xu Chi's Xu
brilliant ghosts who went in and out of the big carved doors
their passion invented a self-destructive history
        'split personality' split again
death's kith and kin   take our group photo
hand-in-hand childhood friends   grew up with the nation

---

59. 'Are you looking for Li Dashu? In this courtyard, I knew him best, Li Dashu
sold this house to my father.' [BH]

60. Cangjie, the legendary inventor of writing, traditionally *fl.* 2650 BCE. [BH]

61. The author uses an irregular plural here. [BH]

62. i.e. the Great Leap Forward, or Second Five Year Plan of 1958-62, the
disastrous attempt to turn an agrarian society into an advanced industrial one in
five years, which resulted in the catastrophic famine of 1959-61. [BH]

6

the Imperial Garden put me up   sent me sightseeing
a flower-picking ghost seeking   from stamen to stamen
the source of the fragrance   with a face meeting a flower by chance
double charms brewing the same drop of deadly honey
on a wet tongue   one night always even more dripping wet

the soun o yir vyce niver stops   och c'wa then   seduce uis
mither's ben the hoose[63]   multiplying outdoors caesarean-like
Edinburgh House is near   Jinmao Tower is near[64]
in layer upon layer of lust, caution[65] will o' the wisps light up chilly shrinking
loneliness   South Gate in Los Angeles?   or any place?

or it isn't anywhere   the shadow of Imperial Gardens
the darker the sweeter   always baring its back to the world
waiting for me   like a festival   like an internal organ
perfuming   the thick white ghost hosepipe says gush
and gushes   can ghosts grow old?   petals die countless times

still holding a baby   mother   use me to be reincarnated
the blackest night is always yesterday   the blackest window
is always a poem   dropping out for a home lost in nowhere
back to where? we are here   shoulder to shoulder
hiding   hearing the citywide traffic roar past the wound

a grey western-style house floats on the sea   also like
a girl at a festival   can't take youth's bloom off
stamens pouting   all along in discussion of beauty
bitter-tasting ash still drifts down by the son's feet
mither   I dreamt of you last night   last night was endless, endless

---

63. Shanghai dialect, 'the sound of your voice never stops/oh come on/seduce me//mother's indoors'. [BH]

64. Jinmao Tower in Pudong, Shanghai, is 92 floors (420.5 metres) high. [BH]

65. *Lust, Caution* (1979) the novella by Zhang Ailing, adapted for the film of the same name by Ang Lee in 2007. [BH]

鹤乡
Crane Land

1

where are the cranes?   as stone steps   narrow paths   grassy slopes
all the way down   groping into midnight and being groped by midnight
penetrating silence and being penetrated by silence
lake faintly reflecting   sky's dimly spreading phosphorescence
the forest is a shadow master   holding and guarding the tiny
wooden pavilion   some crane's neck slowly blows a candle flame
every night sketches the outline of an empty bottle on the table
every night like tonight   spread with longevity   slim
exquisitely carved creatures

where are the people?   blazing amber colours in the whisky tumbler
have condensed the messages from outer space   soak listening landscapes
the little willow's silhouette leans on a screen of crystalline silver waves
shyly dressing   reed beds dream a homeward bound boat
the shore steps into starlight   water lilies coiled snow-white in a bowl
(a painting always newly hung on the wall)   tonight
is everlasting night   sitting beside cranes and deleted to eternity
by cranes   substantial silence in the air   hurls itself in
the window   moves blindly like table end wings furtively flap

this is how longings elapse and are longed for by elapsed time
indulge in this moment and open wide the abyss of this moment   tiny
wooden pavilion   perching beside the forest   beside the night
with a shape of a descent-destroyed bird   that black neck
grey feathers   long steering legs   surround a pair of searching
eyes   drawing the arc of life from the side
echoes this silent thought   oh how hard to write the desolate cries
crane's warm dark guts   down low embrace the world
wade across its own rotten leaves   every place is limitless

2

we never leave the home of calamity
this once and again forces us to take off   forces us to land

a ravaged pocket universe set on a plank pier
lake water folding light and time
an opened book   needs no redundant rhetoric
and skill   you stand there   an unruffled reflection
polished by how many reflections   reed leaves tremble no more
their rustle only arm-in-arm with trembling with thought[66]
this is a moment on the brink   our lake
a whispering azure fallen leaf lying among countless fallen leaves
a sail about to embark has sunk into a voyage
the lake bed denies   plank pier like a chair at the end of the fields
never stops watching over a dead deer leaping into cloud
deserted silence   hoof prints stamped all over the sand

                                        now cries come
cries   one like the waves   one like tree shade
containing a vast expanse and contained by a vast lamenting expanse
an invisible mouth   lifting images of everything
calling to the path we walk the deep woods have just completed their autumn
        colours
calling to a rotten tree trunk   heavy with moss it waits in the rain
to call   gravestones leaning every which way   names returned to stone now
departed souls hide in cranes' bodies   like army uniforms carefully stored
in wardrobes   red stars of mushrooms   silver-inlaid oak leaves
(Tsvetaeva is just fitting *Mountain Poem* into an envelope
sent to a slender blood-red tongue tip   she says   falling in love is not free)[67]
iron bars of cry after cry   locking in the Earth   locking in the journey
no one has ever elapsed   the birds of History
enumerate congestion and nothingness

---

66. Pascal, 'Man is only a reed, the weakest in nature, but he is a thinking reed.' [YL]

67. See Tsvetaeva's *Letters*. [YL]

                                                              now he has come
the lake is there   the empty field is here
a gravel path underfoot   signs point to
a virtual end   a gust of wind rolls up the smell of the dew on his body
we glimpse an old farmer rubbing dirt from between his fingers
a fisherman wading the water to haul in his nets   *'every action*
is embedded in Earth's musical score   every day is a leaf
you watch spiral down as you stand at the window
a golden curled grief   silently mixed with the grief embraced beside tree roots
hence   every crane cry comes from a woken friend'
light like early morning and like afternoon spills on his sleeve
honey-coloured dust also ambling   passing the white poplars
a northern landscape painted again and again   *'there's nothing*
doesn't come through darkness   gives you a version of being a guest in your
        dreams
no need for dictators   to help you analyse the meaning of slavery
the meaning of migration   lyrics futilely encore their wails
you grow inside yourself   freshly green like bracken
carrying an unwieldy reincarnation   every pace treading the impossible
every pace stepping out just so'   crane cries and footsteps
croon language borrowed for generations from the forest library

'Earth's abundance teaches you what simplicity is
leaning over poems like seedling ridges   a kind of full-throttle passion
a kind of full-throttle stability   piano keys press night and day
a site of uncounted deaths clinches a deal with a site of eternal life[68]
will we need to borrow the devil's powers?   History a heart-broken autobiography
lives to be (not written to be)   inescapable drama   our mountain
has turned grey too   our Faust has still not loved[69]
to walk in a line of verse   corresponds to everything refused or endured
simplicity is not a conclusion   it's only an infinite elegance'
wearing an almost bashful smile   the posture of the cranes reconstructed
        as a portrait

---

68. See Goethe's Faust. [YL]
69. See Tsvetaeva's *Letters.* [YL]

3

a clarinet overtakes a crane neck   probes
into the room and a page of a snivelling music score
echoes magically turn into oaks by the window
feathers golden   keeping that convict company

stroke by stroke composing for Time[70]
writing Doomsday   far surpassing Doomsday
the guards' boots march to the metronome
the end   everyone once must solo play

a bird's-eye view of ashes   smoke curling up finely
only weakness will stir the soul   infinity
so sweet it tastes bitter   all around sits sky-blue
waiting still for its own nightmare to début

here cranes are steeped   this death-domain   this close listening
cranes come lightly fluttering   endlessly into exile going
forging fate   the loveliest misery
the lament most understood   Deep Time's agony

not one crane   cranes are everywhere
music chews the cud of a deserted gloaming
looking back at each step   how many elegies squeezing
into this one poem   the only moment that is there

like a barb dripping blood   hooking
the children in a cradle of iron homegoing
nostalgia   rhymes the jail sentence straddling the era
Crane Home   burn a joss stick   lean on ten thousand cloud strata

a blizzard of notes flying precipitously
the final end has come   on an icily gorgeous road early
the final end is still arriving   lines of poetry
with warm armpits have crushed the light

20–26 November 2020

---

70. Messaien's *Quartet for the End of Time* was composed in a prison camp during
WWII. [YL]

大夫，我是你身边一滴水
Master, I'm a Drop of Water by Your Side[71]

1

master   I'm a drop of water by your side
stone still clasped to my breast   fish belly after fish belly
always a nip in the air on the river breeze   and the fallen leaf of a drop of
       water
endlessly tossing and turning   floats down   nestles tight in
a figure still softly reciting   our longings
have pierced us both   a dash of inexhaustible dusk
long ago burst the banks   master   above and below the water
you still walk   periscoping the turbid gloom of a world
nestled into the rise and fall   a water drop in a wavelet won't drown again
all around I hear echoes from our tiny lotus leaf-roofed room

2

master   a drop of water is the dictionary we share
on the Miluo   I feel your slowly chilling viscera
2,300 years   still opening up to us
the orchids you wore at your waist melted into the river's body odour
the quiet bamboo grove where you sat alone   buried deep in spindrift
Xupu's[72] distant hills flickering faint ghost images   like a long sigh
crowd in step by step   red panthers can never catch cassia's westering scent
one death darkly soaks the link to a million dying days
oh master   which here isn't far away?   a drop of water
drills straight down through the hearts we share

---

71. The *master* is Qu Yuan (*c.*340-278 BCE), politician, and the first named poet
in Chinese history, who drowned himself in the Miluo River (in today's Hunan
Province) as a rebuke to his feudal lord, thus giving rise to the foundation legend
for the Dragon Boat Festival. This poem contains many allusions to Qu Yuan's
poetry: Yang Lian regards Qu Yuan as his poetic and spiritual ancestor. Qu is
pronounced *chü*, to rhyme with the French *tu*. [BH]

72. Xupu is modern Hunan, pronounced *shüpoo*. [BH]

3

master   flowing spectres flow with sleep-talk
on the Miluo   cracks in the ancestral hall   Dragon Boat Day every day
    for the fire pits
water surrounds you   water flows into you   motherland
when did it forget you?   Dongting's waves repeat your southern accent[73]
    with every breath
north shore and south gaze at the same beauty strolling up and down
who made you choose the word exile to claim an unchanging past life
and complete today's sacrifices?   master   Zigui[74] is submerged
Ying City's[75] broken jade pendants entered your outpouring verse as you
    calmly faced death
each day a ritual   the crowded ancestral hall sinks ever deeper
a descending river guards the source of all poetry

4

master, I'm a drop of water by your side
tiny   heart-shaped   that non-stop fills and refreshes your fate
a person who erases dates of birth and death can only be like a ghost
coming alive with each drop of water again once   rippling once
my seaside next to your marsh-side   damp brush-prints
forever footprints   a vastness   tread on it and it's empty
yet we trod it and trod it again   asked and asked again
master   what still has no answer is that haggard face of yours
an egret pokes at a lonely long verse   heartlessly
shivering   dammed-up tenderness keeps leaking names white as fish-scales

5

master   a drop of water spawns a devoured river
it is holding in its stomach   the chemistry chokes in our lungs

---

73. southern accent: Chu (modern Hubei and Hunan) was the state Qu Yuan
served. It includes Dongting Lake. [BH]
74. Zigui in Hubei, now submerged under the Three Gorges Dam. [BH]
75. Ying City was the capital of the Kingdom of Chu, now in western Hubei
Province. [BH]

has a fishy stench you can't forgive   our concrete riverbanks
like coffin lids   have nailed shut the paths you walked alone
fragrant grasses you felt closely   your lovely poem   guiding mine
one and only written-down long-known resting place
master   no one can tell the blood that constantly rises from the riverbed
and what then?   2,300 years have gone by like this
2,300 years still about to cave in on our heads
endless eulogies show their teeth   pounce on the silence of riverbed cast iron

6

master   the whole river's tides pour into this night
wait for nothing   because all times converge here
vainly hoping for nothing   because your rage one
spring night   autographed our every spring night
nothing can change a poet's explosively choking lungs
reward a thousand troubled times   these lines that can't ford the river
must be one last line   master   what you have just written
a dead end with no retreat   makes me hug tight the stabbing pain of
sand   the cliff of your shadow counts down to an ancient leap
this line is my own Miluo River

7

master   I'm a drop of water by your side
hearing the words you muttered that day   'just here'
Miluo   native home you chose for us
no need to be born here   need to come back here
to connect with a chanting soul   this homely voice in the waterweeds
anyone who drifts is anybody's   this meter spewed and spewed from
        mouth after mouth
sundried salt in blood   skyline's *old age comes creeping*[76]
only waiting for the question   new as a manuscript page   drifting down
drizzle of dormant pain   master   your love watches over our growth
with mud and tender downy green

---

76. From Qu Yuan's *Li Sao* (Encountering Sorrow), line 63, in David Hawkes'
translation, *The Songs of the South* (1985), Penguin Classics, p.70. [BH]

8

master   a drop of water's germophobia meets you
exposing between the lines   a tenseless vortex
spinning a shape indifferent to disappearing   master
you are in me   and I lie down in your sobbing
transparent billows filter countless lives and deaths   leaving for time
our one and only life and death   a poem's one night
never demands more   your non-existent gravestone and my swimming over
equally rapid   violence and tranquillity in one drop of water
equally dark   alas   a soft sigh with neither end nor beginning
nothing will ever again spill from this identical poem

9

master   is it cold underwater?   cold as poetry?
Sima Qian[77] read and understood   Ovid read and understood
the Black Sea you never knew laps into the Miluo River
in the most ancient stone troughs it surges past line after line of verse
look far   master   your soul in water   your water
one drop enough to let us sail   a lifetime signifying
endlessly far off underfoot   Du Fu[78] read and understood   Dante read
    and understood
this road of wind and wave is the one and only road
this most ardent loneliness   embraces every seashore
every salvaged moon   its gleam lights your reincarnation

10

master   I'm a drop of water by your side
in what language can I celebrate you?
or wordlessly   only a froth-flower   new-formed in the heart
tiny lotus leaf-roofed room   tiny rooms echo everywhere

---

77. Sima Qian (*Qian* is pronounced *chi-en*) *c.*145-86 BCE, the father of Chinese historiography: his *Records of the Grand Historian* set the pattern for all subsequent historical writing in China, including the official dynastic histories. [BH]

78. Du Fu 712-770 CE, regarded as the greatest Tang Dynasty poet, and perhaps the greatest of all Chinese poets. [BH]

unbroken brooding like lovesickness   poetry that never leaves
never snivels about nostalgia   master   your stooping breath
seeps into this line of little waves on the Miluo   astronomy of beauty
the blacker the water   the brighter shines the glow in flesh and blood
     that lights you up
getting us acclimatised to bittersweet longing
a drop of water chases a departed soul   sees itself become legend

---

APPENDIX

Written in response to an invitation from *Thatched Cottage* magazine.

This line of verse is my Miluo River

How deep is the Miluo River? That's almost like asking,
how deep is Qu Yuan's poetry? To put it another way,
how deeply can Chinese poetry reach? Before November
2019 I had never been to the Miluo River, yet at the same
time, wandering the world, I felt I had never left the Miluo
River. Whoever silently repeats the opening lines of Qu
Yuan's *Questions to Heaven*

> Who passed down the story of the far-off, ancient beginning
> of things?
> How can we be sure what it was like before the sky above
> and the earth below had taken shape?[79]

has restored the most basic image of the poet since antiquity,
that of a questioner. From Qu Yuan walking alone by the
edge of the marshes, to us today, who can be flying
thousands of miles every minute, where is there an actual
distance that exceeds the domain of the poet's innermost

---

79. Translation from David Hawkes, *The Songs of the South* (Penguin Classics, 1985), p. 127. [BH]

heart? Similarly, if the energy to question exists, how can poetic creation ever be wanting? I never took notice of the nonsense talked around poetry, such as whether the theme was grand enough or not: poetry can be large or small, but absolutely never superficial or trifling. Ever since antiquity, Chinese poetry especially has always been the vehicle for our historical destiny, ordained to be vast and profound, without changing according to fashionable theories from other contexts. Let me say clearly that for me, this is its glory. The majestic Miluo River, boundless and shoreless, includes the vicissitudes of Deep Time, yet still examines the purity of every drop of water. When I say every poem should be written as if it is the last one, conducting a rear-guard action against each dead-end word, am I talking about Qu Yuan? Du Fu? Yang Lian? Or are we all the same? Is it nostalgia for the lost Kingdom of Chu I'm thinking of? The Cultural Revolution I personally lived through? Or a devastating virus running wild as we speak? Life's dilemmas are ever-changing and unchanging, endlessly forcing us to the same riverbank, allowing me to see that this line of verse is my Miluo River stretching out before me, and how could it ever be the last one? Looking at this, the Master's choice is still our only choice – for the poet, one more absolute leap!

三，长诗

LONG POEMS

一座向下修建的塔
A Tower Built Downwards

Knock on lonely silence to seek sound

Lu Ji (261-303 CE), *Rhapsody on Literature*

                    iron trees · Amazon
is there really an abyss?
a concise statement is
a tree begins with a hand
is copied   dismantled
cast   assembled
a set of scaffolding begins
from a false climb
the iron elevation overtakes the treetop's bushy green
last gasp
non-existent reincarnation cut and stacked
the dead peacock of Amazon's outspread shadow
plucked feathers set one by one into
the transparent blue and white drawers
a knocking   begins from ashes
a vast beauty   begins from where there is no retreat
spins into a hole in heartwood
an amber-coloured negative number
sexuality of the dried-out torso
the sinkholes speak honey-sweet
every silken lustre has been surveyed
folds and furrows   adorn a well
rotten moulds
duplicate a burial high above
downward   inward   a reincarnation too close
turned into plaster   clay   iron
peels off 1:1 scale shadows
virtual 1:1 scale breaths
amber- or ash-coloured
sawing each other in two   twin each other

119

the only tunnel
chisels into the scaffolding-fixed body
a section of a handsome mutilated limb turns round slightly
a pit acknowledging its humiliation
shallow as the human shape   approached like outer space
the only darkness gathers in rust-flavoured birdsong
this vertigo is bottomless
where can this fall still fall to?
history spirals down a split-second path to the grave
from now to now   an elusive desperation hung upside-down
a tower's fictional immensity
overlooks its own fictional insignificance
Amazon leaves that pretend to shine
lift our broken book in motion
screw tight the logic of forgery
irreversible life begins from a welding flame
bitter fleshes   begin from a cast-iron concept
assemble a skin piece by piece   what's touched seems true
the truest impossibility is called aesthetics
a dead tree endlessly strips off image
growth art installs our ruins
it has forgotten pain
it constructs pain
a collapse in the crowd's staring eyes
a waiting hearing waits until the sound of a sigh
cold and calm solitude a perfect match
1:1 coincides in
the solitude of the countless dead who wear other names
ghosts
stand tall
arrive perfectly
chosen misfortune

        funeral portrait of my late father
every eyeblink sucks on the final day   and a last day is endless
Father's gaze is familiar and strange   like a stick
fallen leaves tracing a graceful arc   portrait set on

a candled windowsill   the withered cyclamen is an Eternal Flame
the lonely perfume of daffodils thousands of miles away is an Eternal Flame
a jade *cong* probes a dark brown dusk[80]   spreads up outside the window
the murmur of snow thawing on the eaves   are muttering drops of water
dripping then or now?   wetting then or now?
time's matrix polishes a name into a stone
brings slight differences   a form with hands hidden a metre apart
quietly changes me   Father leans back on arabesques of ash
staring at now from what year or month   weeds out my now
from who knows who's year or month   a face
kinship's buffed surface   only just
pulled out from a million little a square boxes piled high in an ice-cold
        warehouse
another bundle of bones that hisses when it's crunched to pieces
(relatives turn round)   the unbearability made a statue for you
a fine thread of blood oozing in the jade *cong*   Father opens a paper bag
hands me a full room of midnight used up   lets me use it again
thousands of miles away   Father's glance in the lamplight bends over the
        dregs of poetry
Tao Yuanming who you read and re-read lifts bitter-sweet chrysanthemums
Han The Withdrawer withdraws into an ocean he never knew
Li Shangyin is being exposed by an extreme prosody[81]
what classic beauty hasn't sucked on a disastrous present
history   has turned everyone over   exposing this one
activates the music of destruction   this instant   page after page
tiny close-written words   unallowably   can't help
supply a terror of black words on white paper   a clock tick-tocks
caterpillar track rhythms say it's a private matter in the end
a row of water-stains in the eaves   messages left purely and loftily
face a dilapidated moment   Father's lifetime of reading
is hammered into a line of living prophecy that catches fire daily
a poem signifying the well-remembered suffering beauty of a life

---

80. The *cong* (pronounced *tsong*) is an ancient Chinese artefact with a cylindrical bore and a square outer section, whose purpose is unknown. [BH]

81. Famous classical writers: poet Tao Yuanming (*c*.365-427), prose writer and poet Han Yu (768-824), poet Li Shangyin (*c*.813-*c*.858). [BH]

a jade *cong* signifying a tiny piece of scarlet flesh
(is it a heart?) continuing to tremble
Father's creations in fall after fall of anniversary snow in the photo-frame
pile up the broken glass where children huddle outside in filth
more darkness awaits a thaw   more final farewells
collapse inside the eyeballs   in the topic of the last day   I am an
    Eternal Flame
a tower in hiding stands inside of all things
downward narration loses no time   but gains time
lessens none of Father's ailments   but grows into a son's ailments
sprinkles no wine on the ground   but pours it into incessantly-sipping
    drunkenness
poem of death written on a birthday   an amber-coloured hole
elegant as Father   sexy as Father   watches me
1:1 sinks into what long ago ended   never-ended
tongue of golden flame   delicately licking the sense of Deep Time
leaving far away from the vanity and shame of words   return to an
    alienated family
this silent tower   'revolves around a centre of nothingness'
Mu Duo said[82]   who was Mu Duo talking about?   the wall is underfoot
the wall is behind   whistling closes in from all sides
lets me pick out that winter night Father's shape came stepping against
    the wind on snow
continuing to welcome being lost another time   this poem exists here
it is just for giving to   slightly pursed lips guarding the calm of later life
unafraid to tell everyone's story

                Huangtu Nandian[83]
where does a remembered patch of land stop?
a blast of March wind   swirls up dust from the road
mud-brick tan immersed in the tan of its name
endlessly-projected dilapidation keeps its reverse speed

---

82. Chinese poet, *b.* 1972. [BH]

83. In Changping District, Beijing. It means *Yellow-Brown Earth South Village.*
See Yang Lian's note, below. [BH]

an instant of torn springtime   leading the whisper of white poplars
let me see   what I continually have to see
for a lifetime   a man's shadow 'pops out' of a pit of green leaves
a touch of surprise lights her up utterly overwhelmed
a metaphor   leaks life from a crumbly notebook
closed eyes smell the fragrance of mud   it still stops you halfway home
                inward reincarnation   the only reincarnation
the ridgeline of the Western Hills is inset in dreams   some metres underground
four in the morning   sickle snow-bright beside feelings   some metres
        underground
a swollen dead cat in the pond   some metres underground
footsteps   before and behind   around the courtyard wall   white paper
        pressed down
on top of graves   every day the bell dragging the hinges   some metres
        underground
a vertical distance with a limestone well-head for buried-alive faces
holds back rolling eyes   only let me see
the cement horizon locking up an idyll's wedding night
a slow-fired cinerary urn   screws down the lifetime-awaited lid
a stretch of worn railway track pounds toward deafness from morning to night
                final farewell   piled up so softly
coming down from Da Haitou's House Slope   dusk has compacted
embracing Zhu Yongsheng sitting on the doorstep   picture a brand-new smile
don't mind death   don't know death   real-life crows
grab at white snow   Liu Dashan's grudge has gone too
some metres away   windows lie down in dark night
promises my ghost   your ghost   must still flutter   meet
to know each other in a cement wilderness where nostalgia can't recognise
using two below-zero ears   to hear the rotted zero
another street lined with blinking neon gravestones
can't hide a little room unwearyingly floating out profiles
                dried-out reed pond like a swallow
gathers in jetlag   yesterday erased   yesterday only now polished
inward reincarnation brings an existence like first love
always as far as the corner of the eye   glimpsing previous lives
like a snowdrift   thawing once to wake once
collapses even more   still clumsy and naïve as our first time

Huangtu Nandian endlessly torn down is still a work urgently needing finished
sour vomit   a mouthful of concrete bile soaks the years and months
everywhere leads me to the dark green of cypresses in the graveyard north of
      the village
Xiao Wuzi disembowelled   heavy coffins of relatives
carried on my shoulders   an origin   a holy land
                  enduring a damp swirl of water and blood
is there really an abyss?   or is not forgetting just the abyss?
is there really a ruin?   or trampled somewhere
a concrete ground bald and crawling   cut by tongues of weeds
an owl's hooting chuckle is recorded in tonight
recorded to be tonight   my deep remorse emptily tracks me
my homelessness never allows a scrapped springtime to stop moving
is it a kind of blessing being eyewitness to my mature self becoming a
      departed soul?
a village   back turned to a forgetful map   inwardly colonised
some metres underground   constellations of debris bright as wounds
beard and hair greying I walk toward you
                  in love with the shattered total inside my body

            'View of a Fishing Village on an Autumn Day after Rain'[84]
no   thing
is a shape
      my
                  vast   ness
speaks the boundless
            doesn't speak the boundless
                  is already boundless
the brush's thirst like the heart's thirst
cold and desolate as this   seven hundred years of accumulated rain   looks
      like snow
leaden and murky as this   a kind of slowness   no water   no sound
a kind of not going at full tilt

---

84. The poem describes a painting of this name by Ni Zan (1301-74), one of the
Four Masters of the Mongol Dynasty. [BH]

pushes aside all your overlooking
and my storyline   stone clouds drift further away
treetop claws scratch through the diaphragm of fine art paper
a shore or several shores   there is a shore there isn't a shore
to watch time is to watch a person   a nobody
boundless as ever   smell of blood newer and newer
my death invisibly brims over my hollowness
my stillness   washes every second my morbid fear of dirt
a space infinitely severe   seals up the flow of passing time
your densely-packed laments cannot unseal it
(like an ice-cold message)
seven hundred years   decelerates to prick the now
1:1
          the shape of leakage
stone
          a lonely grave
                    tree
                              a puff of lonely smoke
water's demons
          my demons
                    phosphorescence in all your hands
blocks a rotten slogan that watches itself wither
a skeleton beaten into mud can't be unblocked
block the flame's brightness   thick smoke a cast-off damask strip in brightness
a high-flying black bat shot dead can't be unblocked
block the reign-title refusing to change   never-begun kindness
bad luck's black ink can't be unblocked
block the unavenged ghost football field all splashed with the green of
          children's legs
the green of a face blocked by a whistle
on balconies at nightfall that cry of 'phony' can't be unblocked
block the foundering of an island   bring a million dirty glass curtain walls
foundering   Hungry Ghost Day[85] every day can't be unblocked

---

85. Also known as the Ghost Festival, held on the 14th or 15th of the seventh
lunar month, when the gates of the heavens and hells are opened, and the dead visit
the living. [BH]

the image of being engrossed in a painting   engrossed in expunging
a person hollowed out by writing   once imagined the meaning of being
a blank stele made of paper   carved all over with letters there in the sky
few going at full tilt   throat sore with sobbing   only writing not few
    enough
can I recognise myself?   can you recognise yourselves?
the screen ice hacked and hacked again   a fleshy sea anemone behind
    barbed wire
rots to colourlessness   can this world recognise itself?
a sleepless mirror   wipes the worst news away each instant
everything is old and worn-out   and nothing has been forgotten
nowhere to come to
            and nowhere to go
a portrait of landscape
                has betrayed mountains and rivers
                            ripples of departed spirits
    sigh out
                that underwater poem
a life used up in vain has a final draft
water is finished   clouds not risen yet   a horizon that sits in idleness
moves to the corner of a mouth   passion piercing to the bone needs only
    a final draft
painting it once is enough   my Deep Time tells all of you
my blank space tells all of you   reciting an eighteen-part elegy
corresponds to (or confronts) frostbite with no beginning or end
a rough sketch is muddy   enough so none of you can take your eyes off it
to recognise history sheds tears   a heart that never flowed out of a level
    surface
poetry   less than no words   person   stopped where there is no road
a kind of doom for every now   every fall from space made ready
a kind of doom sucks in every fall from space   every now
gently swept away by extravagant   identical melancholy
no   thing
            hears a heartrending cry clearly

      Miluo River, some night (with *Crossing the River*)
this is not a lyric   but a poem of death

126

this very night   the river mutters   the dark mutters
this place as isolated as ever   I'm leaning on two thousand years
that non-existent railing   behind and before
a text like a cliff   the great river read and read again
is impossible to cross   the eyes of unrequited love
arm in arm with my endlessly-renewed knowledge of death
string of lights on the bridge   holding reflections buried
under the bridge   an embankment like a stroll in a tower
night wider than a fiction   river breeze and cold mist
dig a hole in the pervasive rotting stink of reeds
it's just here   it's still here   oh departed soul
fly fast   the other wandering shore is quietly wiped away
my dithering can't cross over   the E banks the Xu banks
a nominal century can't cross over   Wangzhu or
Chenyang[86]   what poem hasn't lived packed with southern tribes?
wading across my brand-new dying and dying again white hair
drowned previous lives summon with no enmity yet blindly
a next life the very same   a predetermined place beyond knowing
beautiful woman   can you ride here on that underworld crane?
water-wetted railing   circles in the tower too
waning lamplight   shines on every Bridge of No Return[87]
this is not a lyric   secluded sentiment of ancient kingdoms is dead
two thousand years of exhaling like orchids   fragile sorrow
what meaning has it for breath stirred into rotten mud
riverbed   ripples a water dungeon   a poetess
weeping as she grows old has what meaning   flesh and blood
surge   this river isn't flowing anywhere
under my white hair there's no one in   collapsed
upper reaches lower reaches there's no one there   the last day in dribs
and drabs   a melancholy tower swallows nobody

---

86. See David Hawkes, *Songs of the South* (Penguin Classics, 1985) p.160, pp.184-85. Two Yangtze tributaries and two locations in Hunan Province, associated with Qu Yuan (c.340-278 BCE), and mentioned in *Crossing the River*, which is attributed to him. [BH]

87. The bridge from this world to the next. [BH]

I hear history walk up and down and up and down like
sloughed cicada skin   discarded echoes an ear-piercing and empty
vortex   the diameter of snap-on viscera   grinds
old age reached in an eyeblink   this decrepit
body isn't anybody's   names listed
gouged-out monoliths   pile up a riverbank of false propositions
death that happens alone   coincides with countless deaths
the sexuality of ruin doesn't care whose it is
a poem fished out dripping wet carries all that is non-human
backwards to forgetting   the only fate left
black sand grasps tight to all the reverses spread on the water
exile and drowning yourself can be had while you wait   once spoken
they're lost   a false death comforts a false life
suicide stories substitute for silted-up bellies
this is not a lyric   these stinking flower-engraved
words   eradicate me with the emptiness inside my organs
eradicate poems without needing to write them   the worst news is at peace
        and good
unspendable Hell Money hoards a lifetime of ashes
inflation of the Underworld's currency[88]   sleep-talk with no escape
beautiful woman   rubbish anniversaries on the starry keyboard
rideable or reclining? a crane's cry splatters
a World of Shades   couldn't be closer   the railing
melts when it's leaned on   a tower we do everything to fix
on Yama's Level[89]   blossoms sacrifice to a fat face
a greasy discipline offering up a fly-blown
happiness   crawls   corpse of nobody is enormous
and numb   endlessly firmed-up by a slogan
lies can't cross over   but who says I'm not
 a microchip of lies?   I will go   I am already
gone   I have no other bank   I am the other bank
in this   phoney poem beside a phoney river

---

88. The paper money burned at Chinese funerals for the deceased's use in the afterlife. [BH]

89. Yama, Lord of the Dead (Sanskrit Yamarāja), judges the dead and rules over the many and various hells. [BH]

Erlitou bronze tripod wine goblet [90]

Jie of Xia said [91]
go back to
gold
residual warmth of a banquet
leave behind
the shape
lips
hand out
waists
shine in the dark
a hidden
girl
three toes
jump en pointe
impractical
dance
all directions
gathered into
an ellipse
snow-white hand
taking
a corner of the museum
dizzy with standstill
graceful
pattern wakes
elegantly
confirm
one casting one notch
buried little sea

---

90. Erlitou culture, named for an archaeological site in Henan Province, was a Bronze Age Yellow River valley culture dating from 1900 to 1500 BCE, which is conjectured to be the site of the semi-legendary Xia Dynasty. [BH]

91. The 17th and last sovereign of the Xia Dynasty was the wicked tyrant Jie (*fl. c.*1600 BCE). [BH]

perfect beginning
neck broken by force
hangs low
bronze's black
eyewitness to sacrifice
poured inside and poured outside
a slice of verdigris a sigh of regret
boundless clapping
carves out
tiny mastoids
starting point
absolutely alone
endpoint Heaven's Will
Jie of Xia said
drink me!
sacrificial killing is a container
melancholy is a container
turquoise
please spectate
my yell
is not in my mouth
my death
is always dying
zero distance scorches
pain's metal
true love like this always
the finer
the emptier
flame is a container
silt is a container
sauntering steps
guard a direction dripping blood
can't sink to the seabed
my sea is bottomless
knocking like this always
pit of every day
confirming

downward
subsidence   is a kind of action
impossible   is a kind of action
museum
the only dark growing shadow
sculpting echo
is a kind of action
Jie of Xia said
it's begun
your ghost
1:1
surplus outflow
inside my body
deathly refusal
to discard
simultaneous damage
CHEERS!

Iron Tree · Berlin
seven long lines fall quietly onto the paper   a seven-layered nightmare
inside a nightmare   a tower
never reincarnated outside a person
a string of substitutes put up scaffolding
climb an endlessly taller dead tree
with crystal clarity feel 1:1 formed
lips   ears   corners of eyes   stand tall to be language
a string of aliases like grammar demolished and resettled
a jade-green dead peacock of the Amazon tosses and turns at every street
    corner
sheds every feather   decomposed into seasonal scars
numbered   cut   duplicated   a pane of glass
inwardly opens numberless transparent levels
little clouds of soft shoots   early spring loneliness
imitates the noise of iron branches and leaves powerlessly withering and
    falling
to build a chill in the air unwilling to struggle free
seven fragments are one fragment   one human form

131

ding-dong bell that doesn't ring memory hangs in a derelict skull
flame that doesn't feel slaughter spits out windows sound asleep
timed-out explosions   endlessly throw shrapnel at
lawns bright and beautiful in the sunshine   picnics and children's legs
don't know the Day of the Dead   only wade into the Day of the Dead[92]
deaths so alike so ignorant   one is another
1:1 creating forgeries of each other
an undisheartened amber-coloured tree hole of the heart
unwearied by digging out reflections of the days   the first equal to the last
unperturbed there's no original   anyone is like an original
a fly buzz-buzzing   doesn't stop at wasted words
but is drowning in wasted words   in a lump of amber
fully-packed time exchanges non-existent time
fully-packed history   prizes and honours nothing but
one person's agony   this cut-off place left for me
has no way out   a rain shower remotely controls a pair of dry eyes
false viewing recognises the pitter-patter of false echoes
like the pot that was dropped from Ai Weiwei's hand   hanging
quiet in Ai Weiwei's space   (art and life can't break twice)
some man hanging on a ventilator desperately carries his own destiny
barricades of vital organs can't be bypassed   a masked city of ocean waves
catches up with the lesson of catastrophe   seagull teargas grenades garishly
     explode
on the sea   a poem burns only for the meaninglessness of life
Kant Street Celan Street   stretch countryfolk's little faces   all for sale
can't go back home   so turn back to a lie I can't leave
muttering to itself of reincarnation is reincarnated inside me
slowly-told long lines tell history both bright
and void   biting the only day from inside
someone is formed tiny by tiny bit from their own negative progress
a poem's window is filled with landscapes that can't pass by
begins with a hand   a big tree's real death isn't afraid to derive falsity
and again derive nothingness   every step overtakes the final void

---

92. Qingming (aka Tomb-Sweeping Day), in early April, when graves are cleaned
and offerings made to ancestors. [BH]

in the sound of Amazon cast iron winds   do roots still have a vain hope
     of sprouting?
at the endless height of forty metres   from what bodies are the mutilated
     limbs hacked?
the metaphor of Father's looking back   reaffirms the impossibility of
     looking back
a vacancy won't alarm the sweeping-by spring colours
the blood-clot purple of the Western Hills is inset into the edge of 1976
escape a step   Huangtu Nandian leans a little closer
its dilapidated ruin is me   a cinerary urn filled with cold hugged tight
the ash-grey revolving door of snowy ground gulps down a human shadow
a thousand ages   need just one painting   have just one painting
Ni Zan's tearless sob incomparably heartfelt   overflowed the vast diffusion
and a poem that sucked the autumn floods dry   the same as the master[93]
I run to and fro on the riverbank because my Bridge of No Return was left
     behind
no vain hope of crossing the river because every day spans a great river
the Land of Shades on two banks holds a drifting life together   a suicide
     jump
lands only on boulders of language   bloody froth spatters
the first cry of surprise drowns without a break in the next cry of surprise
tripod goblet like an obscene axle bound tight to the glass-clinking hands
Jie of Xia said   depraved beauty distressed beauty   die again
still 1:1 duplicates an utterly chilled me
coming down touching the dripping wet tower wall   coming down
I tread the spiral path to the tomb   lose once to blossom once
every pouring into adorning a seductive   penetrating image
no other transcending only leaves reincarnation and transcending inside itself
no other rescue   one hand stretches toward the downward spire
I   all you   two leaping red squirrels on this morning's windowsill
the only elegance just locks this transcending in death
the voice we thirst for never exists

---

93. That is to say, Zhuangzi (*c.*369–*c.*286 BCE), putative author of the eponymous
Zhuangzi, one of the foundational texts of Chinese thought and religion, which
contains a chapter (cap. 17) entitled *Autumn Floods*. [BH]

the root's wrinkles   the stone's wrinkles   catch all collapse
1:1 symmetry with pitch-black perfection
relies on nothing else   doesn't let anything else go   substitutes and aliases
rock a towering   old and sick history teaches me to say quietly
history doesn't exist   exploding instants so precisely   from now
to now   completed loneliness awaits a completed   Father
excavating hands lightly slap my body   all things made me become myself
falling down now   April sunlight falls down like dust
enough to let me feel the fierce sway of a bunch of iron branches and leaves
death's fragrance uses Father's limpid clarity
to inwardly endure an unendurable world

AUTHOR'S NOTE

The title *A Tower Built Downwards* is taken from the title of a full-length interview I did with Mu Duo many years ago. The poem is in seven parts, the inspiration for the Iron Trees in the first and seventh parts comes also from Ai Weiwei's piece *Tree*, for which he took an almost 40-metre tall tree from the Brazilian Amazon, divided up it into blocks and from these made moulds to cast a 1:1 scale replica tree: within it the metaphorical implications of life and art are contained. The second, my father's passing away from an illness on 29 December 2020. The third, Huangtu Nandian, is the name of the village where I was sent down to the countryside in the Cultural Revolution, and which no longer exists. The fourth, *View of a Fishing Village on an Autumn Day After Rain*, is the title of a masterpiece by the 14th-century painter Ni Zan. For the fifth, see my essay *The Poetry of Qu Yuan: the Hidden Source*. The sixth, *Erlitou Tripod Bronze Wine Goblet*, is a bronze drinking vessel found at the archaeological site at Erlitou in Henan Province, and is said to be a relic of the Xia Dynasty, 4,000 years ago. Its form is extremely graceful and elegant, a starting point for the aesthetic traditions of later ages. It is now in the collection of Luoyang Museum. The seventh, Berlin, where I now live, which is also a vast, infinite city. Endless histories are reincarnated in an individual body, and in the depths of the 'I', the Iron Tree is everywhere.

YANG LIAN
Berlin, 2 May 2021

迷宮

Labyrinth

Eternal Non-Being, desire to see its mysteries,
Eternal Being, desire to see its boundaries.

Laozi Dao, *Dao De Jing* CAP.I

Returning to what is destined, that is called Eternal,
Understanding the Eternal, that is called Clarity.

Laozi Dao, *Dao De Jing* CAP.XVI[94]

...even Homer...only one word, and that uncertain

George Seferis, *The King of Asini*[95]

1

this year chilly winds are whistling   damage
deleting   heaping up   images of stones
images of bodies   a burning sun scorches
seizes the vague and shadowy self
a kind of cold random and aimless as fiction
a direction head-butting a wall random and aimless
turns round again   along a blueprint of nothing
treading on dust buried by dust
submerging into the ocean that leaks from the ocean
no overlooking can encompass life's dead angles
stone clan   tree clan   wind-howl clan
level on level   departed souls are boundless urns
detaining me

2

and you   the one in the dark unseen world
walk   behind the thin bronze hedge
sigh   behind the elapsing iron moment
imagined snake hair stretches out its hiss

---

94. Translation BH, following Yang Lian's reading of the text. [BH]
95. Translation Edmund Keeley, *Complete Poems* (Anvil Press Poetry, 1995). [BH]

night and day saying as it rolls and rolls   hold up
breasts of suspense   only naked for ruined eyes to see
do I know you are there?   or do you know
one inch away   who is not distance itself?
an existence hidden in bright day
neither a love nor a history have an end

   3

but here is the exact end   and another morning
restages the instant of birth   has birdsong
trapped by weariness a meaning?
a wall laughs out loud at growing tall   says to me   wrong again
has the dismay tormented by dilapidated ruins a meaning?
14th June 2022   a numb battle scenario
Transposed to the centuries BC   (Adonis says)
beside massacring mouths   chanting mouths
do the days entangle shame or is shame casting the days?
between cries for help and begging   havoc and self-destruction   a sudden
        sharp turn
to sunflower-golden nightmares collapsing and collapsing again
the weariness of the dead is the only true weariness
blood stories   have blocked life   and blocked death too

   4

black hole of melancholy   the invisible thread you passed to me
where is it?   very snowfall is the last one
where is the never to be whitened Earth that catches it?
another trickle of tears drops into the void   eye pits
ancient desire   opening spangled as light on waves
finely twist a glittering thread
where are time and nightmare?
your universe is not my universe
two dangling drops of seawater raise a wet resemblance
what we call destiny   is handed to us
scalds the void   dissolves into a void
so farther and farther
in succession

5

below one time is another time
below one wasteland is another wasteland
this yellow dirt road underfoot   a lifetime walked
still dry   rough   clenched
isolated stone pillars at the start
carved stone flowers open independent of the seasons
at one time this was called the home place   only making me see
a cold moon over the archway   whizzing flung
treetops buckled by cold nights   falling leaves swoop like black bats
in a pale golden moon-halo the souls of palace maids frantically dance
mountains and lakes underground   pavilions   project outlines of
        departed souls
this place so very near   you can touch it if you want
a sea of fire   a bout of weeping   a deafening silence
a long-achieved vanishing fuses into our vanishing
kicked-up shards of brick and tile sprout bits of skeleton
the first line of verse has forgotten the year and day it was written
sedimented ocean waves never splash from stone's entrails
a phantom hullabaloo hidden inside another phantom

6 (non-fiction)

metal doubly silent in a savage blast
Earth's lungs quake   pipelines tremble
shrapnel of mobile phone screens shining and crumbling
outlines every face down in Hell   half human half ghost
deep in the underworld   who isn't like an infant?
a kind of life just birthed by death
a held breath follows the guided missile's whizz
to live is to wait   waiting is enduring
become a tiny tiny insect in a metal spiderweb
filthy air stacks up into a doomsday like raindrops
hunger of banished bellies refuses all bandaging
cancelled nights and days stockpiled in the heart
in the only darkness left   can terror's power supply
light up a poem?   a riddle like ourselves
goggling at incessant internal and external pulverisation

7

as I say we   am I saying you and her?
a sky-blue ocean collages the agate of an instant
soft footsteps pass through a medieval
monastery's midday   wells silent and still
each leaf shuts tight its wooden gate   stares after his back
dappled under the pomegranate tree   a line of letters
blossom on kneecaps not seeking anything
two faint smiles hang unrelated in sunshine
two sisters tesselated into one superimposed look
Isolated, with no before and after (Eliot says)[96]

8

if we know we're lost are we still lost?
coming down a collapsing staircase   everywhere are
crimson potsherds   each like a face
recognising an invisible mirror   does it confirm this thread's
unreadable tourist map has a meaning?
so many feet have ploughed up the dust   every turn
is toward an unfamiliar gloom   yet it's as stifling as ever
what days are not like an entrance to archaeology?
leading me to step onto a decayed   brand-new tomb path
marble thrones the imperial court   concubines' lotus steps that abrade
    the frescoes
a gust of wind alerting the hillsides floods again the indigo of wild flowers
is what we turn back to an identical here?
our room   is unmoved but has changed its number
can't stay in life or death   reduced to a language extinct and extinct again
cicada song so ear-piercing   the end of the tomb path
waits for the sacrificial minotaur to pounce on flesh and rend it

9

the ocean's reflection cannot arrive
inside flesh and blood where the piled-up worst news

---

96. T.S. Eliot, *Four Quartets*, 'East Coker', V. [BH]

mothers flung onto concrete   more iron chains
identical cold   long ago fastened   never to break
January's icy winds still defying me to blow   never deblocked earth
blindly birthing children like blindly birthing poetry
cremation urns and wombs have consented to the same funeral rites
yellow-white arms virtual as a flourish under neon lights
who sees who is false?   or is everything false?
this village has a north side only   on the road to hell
are only coffin-carrying carols undemolishable
dry bones breed dry bones   as weight breeds weight
yet we are weightless   featherlight words
go carrying the world   is everyone outside or inside?
both at once?   hear bodies knock out the gloomy gongs
karma wants us no more   it's nothing but our selves

10

labyrinth of love   labyrinth of history
neither anything but the labyrinth of one's self
a drop of emerald lake water hangs on a delicate earlobe
a little lake floods an ocean
doing all it can to be cast into the immensity of an instant
my surveying the scene chases my getting lost
little by little increasing primitivity and frenzy of a drop of water
where are you?   does the pain of dreams
drip back into a previous life or an imagination?
the powerless pouring back sea   daily renewal
daily extinction into dusk that erases direction
a steel fence blocking off a house door
has completed an utterly isolated world ready for use
with no way out it falls in love with all colourlessnesses in a drop of water
one instant begins to rebuild all the filth

11 (non-fiction)

22nd February 1955
the passport says   birthplace: Beijing
Father's signature and City Hall say
Birthplace: Berne

Swiss sunlight sucking up white snow asks   do I exist?
7th January 1976
117 Block 1 University of International Relations   the 'Ghost Hall' says
corridor gloom[97]   news of Mother's death
fallen on the glass blackboard desk it shattered and shattered
with a little stone bridge   frozen stream   the last lotuses
buried underground   the north wind that blows out of an old photo
    album asks
does weeping in vain embraces exist?
1980 West 2nd Street, Chengdu   a gardenia
perfumes the second button on her breast   the sound of rain at Qingyang
    Palace[98]
with an accordion sob it asks   does beauty exist?
This stone stands as witness for those who can no longer speak[99]
Auckland   survivors and extinct volcanoes
pull an ocean apart   a memorial's solitary
skeleton entrance asks   do anniversaries exist?
a gleaming sea surge   how far out has the boat sailed?
a line of verse gazes after itself   how long has it mourned?
1997 North London's lake entrails shine luminescent
Lee River Valley's departed souls embrace   swans swim through
in watermint's bitter aroma   22 Carlton Mansions
a monster butterfly visits an emptied house
transforms a summer suns' flittering focus
on dark red scaled wings tear-filled eyes ask
do I exist?   does not-I exist? does the question of existence – exist?

---

97. A *tongzi lou* or 'tube block' is a block of flats built around a central courtyard, with rooms off both sides of a central corridor. Homeless in Beijing during the Cultural Revolution, Yang and his mother broke into a university building, and set up home in a classroom there. [BH]

98. Qingyang Palace, Chengdu, the most important Daoist temple in west China, which may be more than 2500 years old. [BH]

99. John Minford's translation of the inscription on the memorial to the Tiananmen Massacre, which Yang Lian and his colleagues made in Auckland, New Zealand, in October 1989. [BH]

12

deaths layer upon layer   death has only one
zero   a snare of nothingness hanging in the sky
a whole family sit around the lamp   the door
warm slippers waiting for feet   little lanes connecting
streets with no one on them   like dry tributaries
do you clear them to zero or do they you clear you to zero?[100]
zero doubled or zero null?
flesh and slogans   overtake the same percussion piece
multiplied times without number still equivalent to a deaf ear
hypertoxic white human shadows in white mist
disinfect me   eradicate me   never there to not there
the snare drops   entrapping each name
bridles   zero reality   zero history   zero I   zero infinite
noiseless unstirring   strangled tongue

13

is there really another shore? which shore is the other shore?
sneak across a river and sneak across a movie made from water
what difference?   the mute girl in the hair salon
works up the lather of terror   secretly photographed Tumen River[101]
police cars   parents shot dead   dark blue night
fake green hills   cut human legs in children's drawings
are chased and arrested) with you   where can you escape to?
wall of water   built for you   taut as skin
collects every informer   this drop that is you
lightly touches underwater   soft kisses   all holding bans
the other shore's refusal the same as this shore   the lens changes
Peach Blossom Land[102]   discarded knows nothing of other lands
you   (and I)   have we sat down in different darkness?
a tear-drenched person   knows only they themself will not wake

---

100. The reference is to China's Zero-Covid policy. [BH]
101. On the border of China, North Korea, and Russia. [BH]
102. A story by Tao Yuanming, written in 421CE, about an ideal paradise where the inhabitants live simple, happy lives, and know nothing of the world outside; it can also mean an ideal rural beauty spot, or an idealistic dream. [BH]

14

a silhouette by the riverside reed beds   round the corner
a tombstone with carefully erased dates of birth and death
lying down among the waves on an island in Venice   round the corner
pitch-dark tomb paths take us spinning
'So it shall go until the end of time' (the Master said)[103]
a vortex of sighs again and again disappears before our eyes
vanishes as if for the first time in a worn-out place
delivers a face of cross-hatched chasms to water's embrace
a fragment of time is a corner   a person
is a montage of corners   turning and turning
under a snow-white blade   losing the way heaps up into a pedigree
a stone castle guarding green valleys
apple trees   homemade wine   stairs climbed in the afternoon
await the final coda of the longest long poem
yet the overlooking eye never arrives
counted   written swallows   with their own time in their beaks
'We who have passed over Lethe' (Pound said)[104]
a corner recognises a coincident vanity
countless corners   embedded in each other   cancel out each other
montaged devastation   stripped bare as love's promises
so time and atmosphere softly separate

15

is the whiff of perfume a dimly-discerned demigod
coming from a gardenia?   coming from imagination?
the whole night through you are embracing   doubled
soaking   body odour's stamen straining your little mouth
burying you in   dissolving you in
bamboo leaves woken by first light   deep breaths

---

103. 'The Master' is Qu Yuan (*c.*340-278 BCE), the first known Chinese poet. See David Hawkes, *The Songs of the South* (Penguin Classics, 1985), *The Nine Songs* XI, *Honouring the Dead*, p. 118. [BH]

104. Ezra Pound: *The Cantos* (Faber & Faber, 1998), canto LXXIV p.463. [BH]

keep dreams   entrails dancing naked
contamination always in a forming world
stirring up the garden on green fingers   sound of rain
soul of silk weaving   weightless wounds
tightly enfold unendurable pain

16 (reading *The Criminal Lu Yanshi*)[105]

this convict book   this criminal book
written in blood ties   words   stab at the innermost heart
this book of bunches of fugitives trembling beneath bridges
this book of tracing relatives' final farewells on brightly-lit streets
a view of someone's back is not a sketch   it is an entity
a forgetting   recalls everything unforgettable
weed-based nutrition screws home the Gobi Desert
forges a nail of hunger   stomach hides shackles deep
and love like an unwearied sentinel
escorts the horizon of daughters   retreats daily further
this book of verdicts quietly blurs months and days
stammers the unlearnable foreign language of politics
our names fill in his name   crimes
axis   drags out two ice-cold rail tracks of coughing
histories of crafty return home shrivel like desire
nothing to do with a wife   or with the direction of falling down shot
tastes refused by a daughter can always be lovelier
and betrayal so flirtatious   daughter born so coquettish
doomsday   this road crazy as fiction
true as fiction   a retrospective book finished long ago
because nothing can be retrospective
an abrupt blank   fallen into the nowhere of dying
brilliantly we merge into him
an embrace awaited in silence

---

105. Yan Geling (*b.* 1958): her 2011 novel *Lu Fan Yanshi*, was filmed by Zhang Yimou in 2015 as *Coming Home*. [BH]

17

all oceans are actually one ocean
ruins of people   lost in the blue
but bluer and bluer   soak our time
never overflowing a human form   Snake Goddesses[106]
have forgotten they coiled into this tunnel or that tunnel
tourists' footsteps   have forgotten stepping into
someone's shade under the low eaves
the ancient ceremony of this or that devastation
coiling and winding through the forest   finely carved
leaning closely into tree leaves in the underworld   radiant and blind
once   arrived at the boundless beauty of losing their way

18 (non-fiction)

we sit in the kitchen at 18 Kurfürstendamm
listen to a bomb in Auckland   Da Kang in New Zealand[1074]
a cloud motionless in a blue sky   in memory
restored as snowdrift   a dead volcano hanging suspended
long downhill paths probe Amazonian tree roots
flesh-pink sighs dug out by Ai Weiwei[108]
opens up bizarre visions in a Mitte art gallery[109]
the perfect helplessness of the poem *Root*[110]
a ceramic ruyi sceptre crawls like a garishly-coloured scorpion
stinging the far North West   father   Wenchuan[111]   a thirteen-year
     silence

---

106. Minoan figurines found at Knossos in 1903 by Arthur Evans, now in Heraklion Archaeological Museum. [BH]

107. *Da Kang Has Something To Say*, a wonderful internet current affairs blog. Blogger Da Kang reports from Auckland every day. [YL]

108. Ai Weiwei (*b.* 1947) contemporary artist and activist, now living abroad. [BH]

109. In central Berlin, on the River Spree. [BH]

110. *A Tower Built Downwards*, see above, pp. 17-18. [BH]

111. County in the north of Sichuan Province, where a 7.9 earthquake occurred in 2008, and where Ai Weiwei was active in leading a citizens' investigation which named the children killed when a school collapsed, highlighting corruption in the building industry. [BH]

children's flesh and blood engender only non-stop weeping
(nightmares metaphysical enough to be so specific)
we sit in the garden of 72 Heerstrasse, Berlin
read *Poems on Turning Back History*   Geling's bag of white clothes[112]
in contrast to the bamboo grove   unbroken green waves lapping Causeway
     Bay[113]
cloud-clothed YoYo drifts over history's gouts of blood
rank and salty thirty years   flow back to today
to this moment   concentrated into thirty-eight degrees
boils Queen's Road[114] to a bone-chilling sweltering summer
Da Kang said and said   yet unsayable foundlings
in crowds   alone   run motionless
same as viruses same as bats   hang upside down in life
the living witness their own defeat and decay
refugee children lie face down on the beach
Vinnytsia[115] mothers beside blown-apart children
(always the children   stumbling again and again over stones)
love and history retreat into the same solitude

19

who is Ariadne? in whose labyrinth
is she at a dead end? love's magnetic forcefield goes woo-woo
but does a poem's bird-head exist?
word and word biting down hard   isolating
seek each other   interminably seek
vast   boundless   north and south poles that rend us
migrant birds fly through time   fly through space
one outlines the other with its cry
this one's departed soul has the other in its beak
my soul   like a song   like tears

---

112. *A Tower Built Downwards*, see above, pp. 95-97. For Yan Geling, see Note
105, above. [BH]
  113. Hong Kong Island. [BH]
  114. Hong Kong Island. [BH]
  115. City in west-central Ukraine, scene of Nazi atrocities in WWII and Russian
missile strikes in 2022. [BH]

a transparent wall orders your arrest   breaks me
love battered and bleeding   seeks the way home
seeks and seeks   the only way home since time began

20

soul in water   sunset glow and water surface
reflect each other   we cross the bridge hand in hand
two thousand years on the far riverbank   five thousand years on the far
    riverbank
an indistinct city trembles in the evening breeze on the far riverbank
does the breathtaking aroma come from waves or skin?
doubled ripples above and below the water
the to and fro of each end restages the conclusion
a bridge like a kiss   steps from this mouth
into that mouth   churns like gills
sunset glow on the skyline turning   water immerses itself
invisible depths   we reflect peach blossom
unafraid that death has undone so many[116]
falling in love with the Bridge of No Return like falling in love with the
    Magpie Bridge[117]

21

so   my   tear-drenched person   this poem
like the Old High Light standing silent on the riverbank (W.N. Herbert said)[118]
looks far out to sea (Homer, Virgil, and Dante said)
a grindstone   (Knossos, the Yin Ruins, and Sanxingdui said)[119]

---

116. Originally from Dante, the line was borrowed by T.S. Eliot for *The Waste Land*. [YL]

117. The Bridge of No Return connects the world of the living with the Chinese post-mortem underworld. The Magpie Bridge over the Milky Way connects the Cowherd and the Weaver Maid on the 7th night of the 7th lunar month, allowing the lovers to meet for one night only. [BH]

118. Contemporary Scottish poet W.N. Herbert lives by the mouth of the River Tyne in a converted lighthouse known as the Old High Light. [YL]

119. The Yin Ruins near Anyang in Henan Province, the largest and oldest archaeological site in China, was the capital of the Shang Dynasty (*c.*1600-*c.*1050 BCE),

soft sighing for the glory days gone in a blink (Li Shangyin and you said)[120]
a disaster the counterpart to a line of verse   countless disasters
superimposed into you and me   a blink and again a blink
this is how a ruin grows in emptiness
an archaeology of flesh   foundation of our terror
is it cleaned up again?   the next shock   the next agony
is it brewing again?   a scratch on stone
that language of glaciers and tank tracks   a world language of devastation
we have been spoken before we were born
after we leave we will continue our outpouring of forgetting
this is no doubt a perfectly ordinary year (I said)[121]
ordinary as death   dark-red sludge infiltrates the sewers
a dim bloodstain on a slice of time
pales into an indelible coincident portrait
a word lives in the labyrinth of a poem
a dead-end since time began   yet it goes groping on and on
a dying day is obsessively cleaned space
infinitely chaotic time included   overtakes the meaningless
without death   would people still dread time? (Yufeng said)[122]
yet does being afraid   carve its heartless beauty stroke by stroke?
oh come   my tear-drenched person   love and history
are equally inexhaustible   interpermeate   invisibly permeate
a self stuffed with countless crumbling strata
no one can leave this labyrinth   but why want to leave?
the stone stairs of this poem descend layer by layer   under the scorching
    sun

---

the first historically and archaeologically attested dynasty. Sanxingdui (Three Star Mound) is a major Bronze Age site in Sichuan Province, dated to the 12th-11th centuries BCE, identified with the ancient kingdom of Shu: its material culture was very different to that of the early Yellow River cultures. [BH]

120. Li Shangyin (c. 813-858), politician and major poet of the late Tang Dynasty, known for his densely allusive poetry, which often deals frankly with erotic or sensual themes. [BH]

121. *1989* by Yang Lian, tr. BH, *Non-Person Singular* (Wellsweep Press, 1994), p.37. [BH]

122. Dong Yufeng, a very talented old friend I saw a lot of in the 1980s. [YL]

tottering steps   twice wade into doom
addicted to a poem   thawed in a poem
reading dumbstruck
the beauty of losing the way surpasses every other beauty

22

a summer passes obscurely into nowhere
in the garden outside the window   birds sing in another time
up and down the stairs   lines of verse assimilate footsteps
that flutter on the carpet   dark and weightless
openly bring all the sacrificed boys and girls back
you are inches away but cannot touch
a first love   makes refreshed hell reveal itself at an address
our words   every archway opening
a darkness inside the door   mooing roars block the throat
does the immemorial ox head have someone else's name?
teeth rip us from inside to outside   we are gobbled down
can we escape into another name?   poetry's obscure and harrowing journey
hears my Ariadne go from room to room
like a dolphin leaps among painted waves
this poem needs no thread because every direction is homewards
from start to start   the beauty of a moment
finds buildings in ruins   illumines buildings in ruins
one summer   a thousand summers   pass into us
reincarnation's bad news opens the perfection of a bird's eye-blink
(like the small grasshopper on the windscreen this very instant
six little green legs and two long antennae   stand by
to resist shattering in the next instant)   perfection of confusion and aspiration
plant love in history   so history is like love
the kinder the farther away   the sum of all labyrinths not far enough away
infinitely seeking   leaping into the urn of a ghost ocean still not enough
you are there   a poem tightens the void
smothers a heartfelt farewell   carries it all
I   an interminable sigh of regret
after a thousand years   innocently turn to you to begin

奥威尔的新年（诗剧版本）

Orwell's New Year

A Verse Drama

TRANSLATOR: The translator of all the languages in *Nineteen Eighty-Four*.[123]

ORWELL: The author of the dystopian novel *Nineteen Eighty-Four*.

WINSTON: *Nineteen Eighty-Four* male lead, who in the end gives up his
　　rebellious plot.

JULIA. *Nineteen Eighty-Four* female lead, who in the end gives up her
　　rebellious plot.

GHOST. The ghost of every sacrificial victim of *Nineteen Eighty-Four*-style
　　reality.

With solo cello, modern dance, art installation.

*　　*　　*

TRANSLATOR:

　　fear of the cold left behind by the cold
　　Winston's mouldy smell left behind by a rat
　　Julia's scarlet sash pulls at the reins
　　on the neck of 'I love you'
　　where is Orwell?　　1984
　　a handful of dry bones time gnawed and left
　　a chill wind growing without limit
　　who is the writer?　　who is the translator?

ORWELL:

　　here is Portobello Road
　　here is Victory Mansions
　　scaffolding of a former home　　drenched in rain
　　as if drenched in New Year fireworks

---

123. I have left *1984* in the poem, as Yang Lian wrote it, though the title of the
novel is *Nineteen Eighty-Four*. [BH]

children goose-stepping past me
a playground where smashed skeletons are buried
memory hole of green grass   that nursery rhyme
records how many huge little massacres?

WINSTON:

or tiny huge massacres?   Winston
is tenseless   a fiction
is tenseless   every day is April 4th
the obstruction goes on hardening every year
my toothless mouth   pandemic dusk
spits out London   Hong Kong   Wuhan
still not thoroughly black   everything has been said
everything must be said once again

JULIA:

no one betrayed me   that pond
grass   elms   enough for all of you
to lie down and lie down again   1984's sexiness
scrolls down to 2021   oh don't stop
the future automatically upgraded in a mobile phone
is a never-invalid denunciation number
I sit up again   a blue hyacinth on my hairline
still sweet as a fake orgasm

GHOST:

I hear the empty voice of the wind speak
but the silent dead should now take the lead
I am left behind and am never left behind
Oceania is not inside time   cemetery is here
the staring prison cell light is not overhead   full moon is here
each dummy in the escorted-away mirror
comes on stage as a phoney   choked-black face is here
a metaphor   drips down today languid and listless

TRANSLATOR:

is it Orwell on the ventilator?

is it Orwell in the Intensive Care Unit?
between tall buildings and high-rises   a head hangs down
is a homegoing bat Orwell?
the virus laboratory waits for a sample
the censorship catalogue waits for your shaggy smile
a disease   gives off the smell of a genome
the ruined witches have ruined Macbeth

ORWELL:

Berlin Wall   Tiananmen   Aids Village   migrant workers
9/11   anti-terror   joint venture   G20   Iraq War
refugee crisis   iPhone   Foxconn workers jump from the roof
Snowden   Assange   Brexit   SARS   trade wars
Chinese Dream   America First   Belt & Road   novel coronavirus
white lung   Li Wenliang   5G   China-EU Agreement on Investment
    Little Red CyberNats
London Great Big Art Exhibition refuses Ai Weiwei   Zuckerberg's
    morning jog in Beijing
who recognises me?   who doesn't recognise me?

WINSTON:

Room 101 isn't death   it's life
a London pub a Beijing 7-star hotel
both use the same sewer underneath the world
the sour stink of Big Brother's piss finds
flesh and blood flushed into the drains in the Square
the rat's squeaking wishes long life
my cage because of me has long life
pale rat teeth bared in my face
this time   even their bite is empty

JULIA:

I am stripped naked like a dirty thought
I must gouge out from your memory
my nakedness   forty years poking my eyes
forty years sleeping in the arms of countless men
and still youth glows   but 1984 is closed

they always come in the night   gun at my back
shooting me back to Orwell's bed
a forbidden wank amplifies my desire

GHOST:

a book wanted the life of every now
2021   China wanted the life of Orwell
he's not here   just like ghosts are always here
common denominator of dust   an instant
crammed full of deleted dead and living
electric flesh and blood can't even howl in pain
what you all recite by heart is wrong
word for word and line by line wrong   the only wrong left

TRANSLATOR:

a pandemic is only a shape
being suffocated is only a shape
another world is still this world
overtake a book   to become a book
what you can be moved into is still a lie
what can't be mistranslated must be a lie
the same mass of cremation flames   extracts
2021   the original of 1984

ORWELL:

sizzling fuming soot
always reality's soot   along with
the satisfied sigh of the next corpse
Big Brother's beefy face   narrowed eyes
embedded in the screen   Room 101
safest   warmest   like the sky
upturning the physiology of cheers
I cheer therefore I have to exist

WINSTON:

that voice says   you are all the dead
Tiananmen tanks rolled over blood-red mud

forgetting buried by wailing is to truly die
burning silhouettes that jumped from New York's twin towers
clouds swollen with hatred is to truly die
a little one-year-old refugee crawls up a beach
a ruined and devastated hometown is truly dead
we   are leafed through to become every funeral portrait

JULIA:

blank   strangled in my kitchen
who remembers Snowden?   who remembers Assange?
Liu Xiaobo died on the evening of a big Beijing thunderstorm
spattering the white hairs on the Thames Embankment
who remembers Hong Kong's snow-bright ocean waves?
those helmets and shields   gave the world a catch-up lesson
on the Cultural Revolution   barbed wire biting into throats before the
     firing squad
dangerous voices must be exterminated first

GHOST:

forget with the newest machines
forget the worst nightmare of waking
we are oh so obedient   cry for help a moment
why are cries for help already forgotten?
the answers are plugged with earwax   the wound of the question
already forgotten   the meaning of froth
is even more a last goodbye still stopping on a wedding night
reuniting with our all-new   shattered names

TRANSLATOR:

in the froth of time   1984 has disappeared
in the froth of life   humans have disappeared
in the froth of language   Orwell's words
are a string of little cracks   what he said
even he himself didn't believe   what he couldn't say
stuck in his throat   a 1st edition of terror
invented once again with every bit of flesh and blood
one POP lightly rubs incarnation out

ORWELL:

    can a long-dead tree root in the Amazon rainforest
    still bring forth new green for springtime?
    self-censored WeChat is blocked as usual
    can the innermost heart escape lethal pursuit?
    the Square is filled with the artificial flowers of children's laughter
    the Money Machine's firefighting hoses shoot in an instant at
    each and every umbrella   profit doesn't go into exile
    the gulf of human flesh ripples in the neon night

WINSTON:

    on a Hong Kong street   my eyeballs are blown out
    in the fishy sea breeze   for one teardrop I am
    wanted   hunted down   escorted into the silence of the whole world
    that non-existent destination   in this
    Black Maria who isn't a political prisoner with no name?
    this sinking ship swallows an unseen depth of water
    little sister's big eyes slowly blur
    night sky is nothing but the ritual that filters departed souls

JULIA:

    even I didn't betray myself   I only
    came back   a waxy yellow face
    always naked   black leather boots changed and changed again
    snow-white breast still like a ball of sludge
    youth's script written to be to shredded
    exposing the nature of performance   *Bravo!*
    in the stamping and cheering   I'm dragged out head down
    to identify a pool of old blood   and the world

GHOST:

    we who are added to a fiction   are powerless
    as a fiction   we who are reduced to imitations
    bob on a boundless ocean of imitations
    a golden life-jacket to save you
    but do you know what to save?
    refugee souls lie face-up on the seabed

noses   eyes full of silt
the coastline of dreams   nebulous as this moment

TRANSLATOR:

Big Brother's victory   is to witness
us competing to be Big Brother
1984's victory   is every year
living a flesh-and-bloodless life
and thus even more thoroughly destroyed
a translation's victory   is never to be revised
the Karma being banned   being burned
throwing out this paperweight of a life is oh so easy

ORWELL:

mobile phones light up like wisps of twinkling ghost fire
shining on your kisses   embraces   lovemaking
anonymous letters of denunciation sent from beside you
as if they fell from the sky   selling out
the bitter laugh in every front-page headline
you all live inside pretty slogans
look around   disasters are always someone else's
weep   my sympathy is like my ravaging

WINSTON:

Winston is Winston's ghost
walking a deserted Oxford Street in London
walking Wangfujing Street locked behind iron bars in Beijing
walking 5th Avenue in New York where rats ramble
the azure sky wiped clean of the stains of flights
a rinsed bottle   this world
broken wings overtake the rituals of weightlessness
perfectly coinciding with being murdered itself

JULIA:

Julia is Julia's ghost
who does a poem cry to for help?   as poetesses
locked up in dungeons   have wept and wailed enough

to see only now that tears are the frailest of animals
spring flowers and autumn moon are shackled too
clothes stripped down to naked skin
naked skin stripped down to a rancid stink
a daily cliff edge   jump then   dummies

GHOST:
virus and New Year both far from enough
a bed retains the imprint of the dead
a glass stove-door divides strange inmost hearts
a crow-black rose   final
freeze-framed life escorted away
awarded to the lie of life   we
used to think some meanings evaporate easily
like smoke or cloud   oh let's fall in love with Hell

TRANSLATOR:
Hong Kong is burning   the world is watching
adverts in Chinese like Cultural Revolution slogans
everywhere Eurosport stuck up   the Party has headed the ball into the net
locked into a cycle of morbidity   Assange
where can a rebellious orphan flee to?
Ai Weiwei or Orwell said
rat's teeth polished snow-bright by indifference
cowardice and degradation have no end

ORWELL:
baby   trampling the second hand of another coming day
quiet days   days that want no jailbreaks
Room 101 embraces doors without number
and the very same instant   makes greed and terror
outstandingly delicious   a written judgment
on a tangled bed   a used-up dream
never lacks enthusiasm   history's broken book
a 1:1 match to be you and me

WINSTON:

    war is peace   this war that massacres
    our selves is one with the deaf and dumb
    freedom is slavery   this freedom to betray
    humanity with no qualms orders the bending of the knee
    ignorance is strength   see pain as
    fiction   then dominate the vacuum of the cosmos
    New Year needs no Big Brother
    New Year needs no Orwell

JULIA:

    New Year needs no 1984
    has resurrection any meaning?   the question is
    do we know what has died?
    accept your then you don't care that life is play
    here is the golden country   twisting the past
    and future   a script that can't be performed
    acts a gang-rape scene every day
    Doomsday like an orgasm   say it and it will happen

GHOST:

    no need to bear it   only enjoyment left
    a seamless prison term is dancing the Square Dance
    the executioner beheads bubble skulls
    POP they shatter like you and I   dead fish
    choke the deep sea where Mothers look back
    we pretend we forgot stifling and sink
    this bottomless poem   has violated all poems
    Orwell's one whistle   fills a howling dreamland

CPSIA information can be obtained
at www.ICGtesting.com
Printed in the USA
JSHW020203250723
45298JS00008B/61